how2become.com

Police Detective Constable: Direct Entry

www.How2Become.com

Orders: Please contact How2Become Ltd, Suite 1, 60 Churchill Square Business Centre, Kings Hill, Kent ME19 4YU.

You can order through Amazon.co.uk under ISBN 9781912370344, via the website www.How2Become.com, Gardners or Bertrams.

ISBN: 9781912370344

First published 2018

Copyright © 2018 How2Become.

Typeset for How2Become Ltd by Gemma Butler.

Disclaimer

Every effort has been made to ensure that the information contained within this guide is accurate at the time of publication. How2Become Ltd is not responsible for anyone failing any part of any selection process as a result of the information contained within this guide. How2Become Ltd and their authors cannot accept any responsibility for any errors or omissions within this guide, however caused. No responsibility for loss or damage occasioned by any person acting, or refraining from action, as a result of the material in this publication can be accepted by How2Become Ltd.

The information within this guide does not represent the views of any third-party service or organisation.

CONTENTS

Hello, and welcome to *Police Detective: Direct Entry.* In this guide we are going to give you a full breakdown of how to join the police as a Detective Constable, via the new Direct Entry programme. From application form all the way through to assessment centre and interview, this book contains the very best advice available for aspiring candidates to the Direct Entry programme.

What Is Direct Entry?

Direct Entry is pretty much exactly what it says on the tin. It's a way of directly entering the police as a detective constable. Usually, you would need to gain a few years of experience with the police in order to progress up to this rank. However, now the police are offering talented candidates the chance to enter the force at this rank, and then progress from there.

If you are successful in applying for Direct Entry, you'll start out as a trainee detective constable, under a two-year probationary period. The training will be suitably intense, with visits to operational police facilities and working within Criminal Investigation units. During your two-year period, you'll need to complete the National Investigators' Exam, and a Detective training course. Once the two-year period is up, you will be granted the rank of Detective Constable, and assigned the rank of Detective Constable.

Whilst working as a trainee, you'll be assigned cases such as burglary, hate crime, sexual assault and fraud. Initially you'll start with smaller crimes, before working your way up to serious issues.

What is the application process?

Given the enormous value of a place on the Direct Entry course, the police are naturally selective about who gets in! In order to identify the best possible candidates, there is a long and difficult selection process. The process is broken down as follows:

- Online application form.

- Police Constable Assessment Centre.

- Online verbal reasoning test.

- Detective Constable Assessment centre, Day 1, and Day 2.

In this book we have broken down each of the above sections into separate chapters, to ensure that you gain a full understanding of each stage and what it entails. In order to pass the verbal reasoning test, and the assessment days, you will need to prepare extremely thoroughly. In this guide, we'll give you multiple opportunities to do this, through practice questions and answers.

Now that we've had a brief look at the application process, and how we'll tackle it, let's get started with the guide.

What is a Detective Constable?

In order to succeed in the application process, the first thing you need to do is to learn about the role itself. So, what is a Detective Constable, and what do they do?

A Detective Constable is a high-ranking officer in the police force. The role of a Detective Constable is to participate in difficult and complex criminal investigations, interview victims of crimes (and suspects), and play a leading management role within the police.

When working as a Detective Constable, your responsibilities will include:

- Directing and participating in criminal investigations.

- Assessing a range of information and data, to come to accurate decisions.

- Developing strategies for managing investigations, and evaluating existing strategies to determine how they could be improved.

- Using the latest technology, to assist ongoing investigations.

- Making cost-effective decisions, with the police budget in mind.

- Ensuring that interviews and interrogations are carried out with the utmost professionalism.

- Participating in, and conducting, interviews with victims, witnesses and suspects.

- Working closely with fellow police employees, to provide the best possible service to the public.

- Liaising with employees from partner agencies.

- Maintaining your own professional standards.

Naturally, this is all pretty difficult! The police won't expect candidates from the Direct Entry course to just walk into the job and start solving crimes. You'll be given extensive training to prepare you for all this, and to make sure that you are ready for the challenges ahead.

Detective Constables are expected to operate under what are known as 'building blocks'. These building blocks essentially underline the way in which you will work as a Detective Constable, and they will be especially useful when you sit the assessment centre. Think of these as a framework or structure for how you would tackle tasks when working in the police:

Preserving Life. This should be the immediate priority for any person who is sent to a crime scene. First aid should be provided to any victim in need, and an ambulance should also be requested if necessary. Preserving life should be the mandatory first protocol, even if it risks tampering with the crime scene.

Preserving the Scene. Your next priority should be in preserving the crime scene. You need to look at the crime scene as an area, and secure all routes to and from the scene, by placing tape over the entrances, assigning officers to guard entrances and deny access from civilians. You also need to ensure that steps are taken to secure physical evidence, without disrupting or damaging this evidence.

Securing the Evidence. Following the above, it's imperative that you take steps to make sure the evidence is handled carefully. This could be in the form of taking witness statements, or even seizing crime scene items.

Victim Identification. Next, you need to make identifying victims your priority. By doing this early, you stand a better chance of identifying suspects, and in doing so solving the case.

Suspect Identification. Finally, you need to engage in identifying and arrest suspects. This is extremely important, as suspects could pose a risk to others, or destroy essential evidence before it can be seized by police.

Core Competencies

On top of this, in order to behave in an exemplary fashion, Detective Constables will need to adhere to the **core competencies** of the role. Core competencies are essentially a set of behavioural guidelines, which you are expected to demonstrate whilst working in the role. Below we've listed the core competencies that would be expected for candidates on the Direct Entry programme:

Emotional Awareness
The first competency on the list is emotional awareness. Emotional awareness is extremely important for Detective Constables, and indeed for any police employee. As a member of the police force, it's crucial that you can learn to understand the needs and feelings of your colleagues, and your own emotions. Part of doing this is your ability to listen to others, making a genuine attempt to empathise with them and appreciate their viewpoint.

Emotional awareness also means that you are able to control your own emotions when under stress. It's important that police officers can remain calm under pressure, as this will impact upon your decision making, and your conduct. Communicating with colleagues in a calm, polite and respectful fashion is vital to your ability to do the job.

A person with emotional awareness can:

- Empathise with their colleagues, taking into account the views of others when making decisions.

- Understand and appreciate the reasoning behind other people's views and opinions.

- Manage their own emotions when under pressure.

- Promote the benefits and value of diversity.

- See situations from a variety of different perspectives.

Positive Drive

Positive drive is all about being the change that you want to see. It's about being a force for positive development within the police, and motivating others to improve their own working practice. You must take a positive and enthusiastic attitude to your work, keeping other colleague's spirits up. As a leader, you must be decisive and proactive, showing a confident and assertive attitude. It's extremely important that every single employee of the police is capable of adapting to new working methods, and constantly improving. Criminals are becoming more and more intelligent in their attempts to evade the law. The use of modern technology has aided criminals in this regard, but it can also aid the police. Using the most up-to-date methods, you will be responsible for tracking down and detaining criminals.

As a Detective Constable, you will be placed in a leadership position within the police force. This means that it is your responsibility to motivate the members of your policing team, and to encourage them to improve and perform the best possible police work at all times.

Along with motivating others, it's also important that you have the drive to succeed The police are looking for individuals who are driven by the idea of perfection, working to the highest possible standards, and safeguarding the public.

A person with positive drive can:

- Understand the need for constant improvement when working in the police.

- Motivate and manage others to improve their own working practice.

- Exercise self-management techniques, to get the most out of themselves.

- Understand their own limitations, and identify areas for self-improvement.

- Give 100% of their effort, on every single shift.

- Believe wholeheartedly in the values and priorities of the police.

Resilience

Resilience is an extremely important quality for Detective Constables to have. Working in the police is an exciting and hugely rewarding career, but it is also extremely challenging and can push you to your limits. In order to succeed, you'll need to be a resilient person. You must be able to face challenges and hardships with an open mind and a calm approach. Obviously, the police do not expect you to be a robot – they know that their employees are human beings and that some of the things you'll experience when working will have an emotional impact. However, it's imperative that the police know you can handle this. They don't want to hire someone, only to have them drop out a few weeks later because they can't deal with the difficult aspects of the role. So, with this in mind, it's important that you are resilient.

Being resilient doesn't just apply to the more difficult elements of the role. It's not just about being able to handle hardships, but it also relates to how persistent you are as a whole. If you are a Detective Constable, then you will be placed in a leadership role. You must be able to cope under pressure, taking decisions for the good of the team, and not folding in the face of disagreement. Also remember that there is a fine line between being resilient and being stubborn. If you want to be a successful Detective Constable, then you'll need to find the right balance.

A person with resilience can:

- Maintain a positive mindset, even when faced with hardships and difficulties.

- Deal with pressure in a calm and logical fashion.

- Provide leadership and motivation for their colleagues and teammates.

- Remain determined and committed to great police work, even in the face of difficulty.

Team Working

Teamwork is extremely important when working in the police. Your ability to work in synchronisation with your colleagues, to create an effective and organised policing unit, will be paramount to the success of the force. The better police staff can work together, the stronger the level of care that you can provide to the public. Policing is not a one-person job. It takes the combined efforts of the entirety of the police to fight crime successfully. As a Detective Constable, you will need to call on the help of many other specialists working within the police, and in outside agencies, so it's essential that your teamworking skills are top notch. You'll also be a leader, required to manage teams, so it's vital that you have an understanding of how to work with others.

A person with team working skills can:

- Develop good professional and personal relationships with colleagues.

- Participate in group activities and team based exercises, playing an important role in these endeavours.

- Take the views and opinions of others into account, and is prepared to discuss the views of others in a polite and amicable fashion.

- Utilise an open, honest and supportive approach when assisting other colleagues.

- Accept that not all tasks need to be completed solo, and ask for help when appropriate.

Communication

Communication is incredibly important when working in the police, and therefore it is essential that candidates for Direct Entry can demonstrate an ability to put across their ideas in a clear and concise manner, in both written form and verbal. Working in the police will put you in contact with a wide variety of people, from different backgrounds, and therefore it's vital that you can communicate effectively. Not only will you utilise your communication skills when dealing with members of the public, and with your own team, but you will also need to communicate with different members of the law enforcement team, and professionals from outside of the police – such as social workers or lawyers. You may also be asked to appear in court, where you will need to communicate verbally. Alternatively, your written reports could be used in court as evidence. These are just some of the many reasons that communication is essential for Detective Constables.

A person with good communication can:

- Communicate effectively, in writing and verbally.

- Identify when it is appropriate to use certain styles of communication and language.

- Adapt their communication according to the individual(s) being addressed.

- Use grammar, spelling and punctuation effectively and correctly.

- Listen carefully when they are being spoken to, taking note of essential information.

- Influence the behaviour of others, in a positive way, using good communication.

Professional Approach

As a Detective Constable, it's imperative that you can take a professional approach to your work. The police are role models in society. They need to set an example, and this is especially true for high ranking officers – such as Detective Constables. The public look to the police for guidance and reassurance, and you can only provide this to them, and build up a level of trust, by acting with the utmost professionalism.

You might be familiar with the term integrity. A Detective Constable with integrity is someone who can act with decency, honesty and kindness, whilst still upholding the values and beliefs of the police service. Your professional standards are incredibly important.

Taking a professional approach isn't just limited to being a decent and professional person. It also means that you take a professional approach to everyday tasks too. It means giving 100% to every single task, dedicating yourself to police work, and working hard to ensure that you stay in top physical condition.

A person who takes a professional approach can:
- Act with integrity at all times, both when working and when off duty.

- Uphold the police professional standards.

- Behave in a way that is fitting of a Detective Constable, showing honesty and decency.

- Be held up as an exemplary role model for how officers and members of the public should conduct themselves.

- Work hard to ensure that they stay in good physical and mental condition.

Investigative Mind
Naturally, this is one of the core skills for any Detective Constable. The clue being in the name – detective! Having an investigative mind means that you are someone who can think analytically about your work, deciding on factors such as investigation planning and how the investigative process will be carried out. Since you are a Detective Constable, this will form one of the key parts of your role, so it's crucial that you can lead these initiatives. Furthermore, you'll also be involved in improving the way that future investigations are conducted, through using self-evaluation and team evaluation to determine what worked well, and what didn't.

At all times, you will need to think logically but creatively, coming up with alternative solutions or methods where others have failed, whilst still maintaining the highest possible standards.

Remember too, that you also need to be open to the views of your colleagues. Just because you are a Detective Constable, it doesn't mean you have to come up with all of the ideas by yourself. You will find that the views and opinions of your colleagues are extremely useful, and could lead you to pursuing methods that work out well.

A person with an investigative mind can:
- Take an analytical approach to investigations.

- Take ownership of decisions relating to investigations.

- Play a significant role in the planning of investigations.

- Seek feedback and evaluate the strengths and weaknesses of different investigative approaches.

- Consult with colleagues to ask for advice, opinions and feedback.

Learning

No matter what rank you are in the police service, you will always be learning from your experiences. It's essential that Detective Constables can learn and grow from each and every investigation. Every single person, in every walk of life, makes mistakes. Whether these are major or minor, it's important that you can learn from these mistakes and improve for the next time. Whilst your initial training will prepare you for the role, at the end of the day it can't prepare you for every single eventuality, and therefore you need to be able to think on your feet and develop strategies for dealing with unexpected scenarios.

This is not an easy role. Working as a Detective Constable will require you to give 100% of yourself every single day. If you aren't learning from your experiences, then you will have a big problem, because improvement is a key part of doing this job successfully.

Learning also applies to your attitude. In order to work for the police, you must be someone who can take a positive and enthusiastic approach towards learning. The police are looking for candidates who are eager to improve and better themselves. Not only should you be looking to learn from others, but you also must be able to take initiative for your own learning and improvement.

A person with good learning skills can:
- Learn from their mistakes, and improve their practice for future investigations.

- Take initiative for their own learning and improvement.

- Demonstrate an enthusiastic and committed attitude towards learning.

- Seek feedback from others on their development.

- Accept that mistakes happen, not just to you but to others as well.

Why Are The Competencies Important?

At this point you might be wondering why these competencies are important. After all, you haven't got the job yet. Well, the competencies are actually an essential part of the job application process. During the selection process, you will need to demonstrate these competencies at every single stage. The assessment centre exercises will be a test of how well you have researched and understood these competencies, and how many of them you can exhibit. Core competencies are becoming more and more commonplace in all job application processes, as employers look for a structured guide on how their employees should behave.

If you are applying to the Metropolitan Police, you will also be judged against the Metropolitan Police values, which are: Integrity, Professionalism, Compassion and Courage.

With this in mind, it's vital that you study up on the core competencies as thoroughly and as early as possible. The better you understand them and how they apply to the role, the more chance you have of gaining a place on the Direct Entry course.

Now that we've covered the competencies, let's move onto the first stage of the selection process – the application form.

Direct Entry: Application Form

The first stage of application is to fill in an online eligibility form. Naturally, the police are highly selective about who they allow into the service, and therefore there is quite a wide range of criteria that you'll need to meet. Here's the eligibility criteria that you'll generally need to match if you want to gain a place on the Direct Entry programme. Bear in mind that certain forces might have different eligibility requirements, so be sure to check up with your local police service first, if you think there's anything which could harm your application.

Education. In order to be eligible for a place on the programme, you must have a GCSE in English Language, of grade C or higher. The police will also consider other higher academic achievements, or overseas English Language qualifications. Along with this, you must have a level 6 degree, or you must be an undergraduate who is expecting to achieve this. Later on in the process, the police will require you to show evidence of this.

Age. You must be at least 18 years old when you apply. The upper age limit is 57 years of age. The compulsory retirement age for police employees is 60, meaning that you would have two years of probation following employment, and then 1 year of service (assuming you apply at the age of 57).

Business Interests. The police take the business interests of their employees very seriously. You'll need to disclose any business ventures that you are currently involved in, or that you would continue to pursue following employment with the police. The business interests of your relatives are also important. If you, your partner or any relative currently owns a shop or works for a business that requires a license – for example, gambling – then this could present an issue, and you will need to declare this in the application form.

Cautions and prior convictions. Past cautions and convictions could prove to be a big barrier for you when applying, but they don't necessarily disqualify your application. The police will look at each case individually. However, here are some crimes which will automatically disqualify you from application:

- Any offence committed from the age of 17 or older, which involved corruption, serious violence, abuse of children or drugs.

- Any offence that resulted in a prison sentence. This includes suspended sentences or deferred sentences.

- Murder, manslaughter, kidnapping, GBH, ABH, indecent assault, rape, burglary, fraud, abuse of children, possession of class A drugs, and supplying of any kind of drug.

Along with this, you will also be disqualified if you have ever committed any of the following motoring offences:

- Dangerous driving causing death.

- Reckless or dangerous driving (within the past 10 years).

- Any offence of drink driving (within the past 10 years).

- Other serious motor based offences within the past 5 years, such as driving without insurance or without a license.

- Over 3 traffic convictions, or 6 penalties, within the past 5 years.

- One or more convictions for regulatory offences within the past 5 years.

You can find a full list of offences which might disqualify you from application, via your local force's website, or via the college of policing.

If you fail to disclose any cautions or criminal convictions to the police, then it is likely that you will be found out and your application disqualified.

Eyesight Requirements. In order to work as a Detective Constable, you will need to meet the police eyesight standards. These are as follows:

- For distance vision you will be 6/12 with either your right eye, or your left eye. You must be 6/6 with both eyes together. If you are someone who wears spectacles or contact lenses, then you'll need to reach 6/36 without the use of these.

- For near vision, you must be 6/9 using both eyes together

- For colour vision, the police do not accept the use of colour correcting lenses, and you will be ineligible to apply if you suffer from severe colour vision deficiencies.

- If you have had eye surgery in the past, then radial keratotomy, arcuate keratotomy or corneal grafts will disqualify you

Past Applications. Candidates can only apply to a single police force at any one time. If you have previously applied unsuccessfully, to any other police service, then you will need to wait 6 months before re-applying.

Tattoos. The UK police have fairly strict rules on tattoos. If you have a tattoo which could be considered as offensive, violent or discriminatory, then you will be rejected. Likewise, any person with tattoos on their face, neck or hands, will also be rejected.

Now that we've covered the eligibility criteria, let's move onto the application form itself. Please note that while we cannot supply you with the exact questions that you'll see on the application form, the layout of the form is likely to be highly similar to the below:

Section 1: Personal Details
In this section you'll need to provide the police with basic background details on yourself. This will include information such as your full name, address, telephone contact information, national insurance number and email contact. You will also need to provide the police with all previous addresses during the past 10 years of your life. If you had a partner living or staying with you at said address then you will need to tick a box acknowledging this.

Section 2: Prior Service
In this section of the form you will need to acknowledge whether or not you have been a member of a police force before, or have served with HM forces or any other nation's military. If so, you must fill in the details of this. You must also include the details of any other government service work that you have taken part in.

Section 3: Previous Application
In this section, you'll need to elaborate on whether you have ever unsuccessfully applied to join this police force, or another force. If so, then you will also be required to explain why you were unsuccessful with your application.

Section 4: Prior Vetting
In this section you'll need to explain whether you have ever been the subject of a previous vetting procedure, by any other organisation.

Section 5: Family/Domestic Circumstances
In this section of the form you'll need to fill in details about your close family. This includes details on your parents, step-parents, guardians,

brothers, sister, step-siblings, children, step-children or adopted relatives, along with any other person who lives with you – such as a flatmate, tenant or landlord.

You'll also need to list your spouse, partner or civil partner, as well as your long-term status with this partner. You'll need to tell the police when your relationship with your partner began, and also include details on any previous partners from the past 5 years of life, with from-to dates on when the relationships started and finished.

When filling in this information, you'll need to use full names for every person mentioned.

Section 6: Personal Character
In this section you will need to disclose whether you have any of the following:

- A current investigation being conducted against your name, by the police or any other law enforcement body.

- Any pending court appearances, in relation to criminal charges. This includes any pending cautions or charges that would require a court appearance.

- Any past military disciplinary measures that were taken against you.

- Any disciplinary or misconduct charges resulting from previous occasions when you served in a police force.

- Any other disciplinary measures that were taken, or are in the process of being taken, against your name, by any other professional body.

Section 7: Acquaintance History
In this section, you will need to disclose any criminal convictions, warnings or cautions that have been made against those who are connected to you through family or relationships. Although convictions from these people will not automatically exclude you from joining the police, they could have an impact.

Section 8: Financial History
In this section, you'll need to list some details about your financial history. It's very important that candidates to the police are in a financially stable position. The reason for this is that officers who aren't in a financially stable position could be subject to exploitation by

criminal groups – who are known for coercing individuals into providing them with access to confidential information. It's important to note too that just being in debt is not the issue, as the police understand that this is normal, but the key thing is that the debt is being managed in a responsible way.

First, you'll need to specify whether:

- You've ever had a credit card withdrawn, or an account defaulted.

- You've ever been the subject of a Trust Deed or Individual Voluntary Arrangement.

- You've ever been the subject of an arrestment of earnings order.

- You've ever had a loan arrangement terminated by your bank or a building society.

- You've ever been subject to repossession proceedings.

- You've ever been registered as bankrupt, or in sequestration. Applicants to whom this applies will only be considered if a period of three years has passed, since discharge of the debt. The same applies to Debt Relief Orders.

- You've ever been the subject of a Debt Management Plan, Debt Payment Programme or Debt Arrangement Scheme.

- You've ever been the subject of a negative court judgement, based on financial issues.

If any of the above apply, then you will need to provide details, figures and dates. You should study your force's website for more information on how your financial status could impact your application.

Following the above, you'll be asked to specify your current financial commitments. For example, current or joint debts, mortgages, credit agreements and credit cards. Finally, the form will ask you to give an honest answer as to whether this debt is manageable or not.

Section 9: Business Ventures

In this section, you will need to list any outside business ventures that you are currently taking part in. Certain business ventures, from you and your relatives, could present an obstacle to joining the police. The form will ask you the following questions:

- Are you currently involved with any job or business interest, which you would intend to pursue following your appointment as a police officer, or a member of police staff?

The second question applies only to candidates who are applying for the role of police officer, and is as follows:

- Do you, your spouse or any relative currently living with you, own a shop or work for a business which requires a license – for example gambling, or the sale of liquor?

If the answer to any of the above questions is yes, then you will need to provide the police with full details.

Section 10: Competency Based Questions
Finally, at the end of the application form, you will be asked some competency-based questions. There will 4 questions in total. While the rest of the form is basically a case of giving the police personal details and information about yourself, here you will be seriously challenged, so it's essential that you take your time and get this part right. If you aren't familiar with the concept of competency-based questions, then here's a breakdown of what they are and how to answer them:

Competency-based questions are questions which are focused around the core competencies of the organisation. In this case, we know that the core competencies for direct entry, are as follows:

- Emotional Awareness
- Positive Drive
- Resilience
- Team Working
- Communication
- Professional Approach
- Investigative Mind
- Learning

However, there is also a chance that you might be asked to answer questions focused around the regular police competencies too. These are:

- Public Service

- Openness To Change

- Service Delivery

- Professionalism

- Decision Making

- Working With Others

Competency-based questions will usually ask you to demonstrate a time when you have previously shown this behaviour. So, you might be asked, 'Tell us about a time when you used teamwork to resolve a difficult issue.' When answering questions like these, whether it's in the interview or in the application form, you should use the STAR method of response.

Below we have outlined the fundamental principles of this:

Situation: Start off your response to the question by explaining what the 'situation' was and who was involved.

Task: Once you have detailed the situation, explain what the 'task' was, or what needed to be done.

Action: Now explain what 'action' you took, and what action others took. Also explain why you took this particular course of action.

Result: Finally, explain what the outcome or result was following your actions. Try to demonstrate in your response that the result was positive because of the action that you took.

Don't give an answer that relays what you would have done or what you should have done, tell them what you DID.

Furthermore, at the end of your responses, always try to tie the answer back to the role itself. For example, after you've finished telling the assessors what you did and how it helped, show them that you know this is important for the police, and why.

Alternatively, you might be asked, 'It's very important that Detective Constables can show a positive drive. Why do you think this is, and would you say that you are someone with this quality?' In this case, you just need to explain what you've read about the competency, and then relate it back to police work.

When answering these questions, you can expect to be given a word limit – normally of about 200 words. This means that you need to be focused and concise when responding. Make every word count, and don't ramble.

Below we've listed some sample questions and responses, to give you some idea of what to expect and how to answer. We've given you 2 questions using the Detective Constable competencies, and 2 questions using the normal police competencies.

We've also left a space in which you can place your own answer, before comparing it with ours.

Q1. In 200 words or less, tell us about a time when you have demonstrated your resilience.

Sample Response

Whilst working in my previous role, as a receptionist at my local convenience store, I was faced with a very difficult situation. A customer had come to my colleague, complaining about the fact that we weren't stocking a particular item. I noticed that the man was becoming very abusive towards my colleague. After berating the staff member for several minutes, he then used a racially disparaging remark. My colleague seemed extremely upset by this.

I immediately intervened in the situation, and informed the man that he needed to leave the store at once. He refused, saying that I needed to explain why the store didn't have the item he wanted. I informed the man that his choice of language towards my colleague was utterly unacceptable, and that he was to leave immediately, or I would call security to deal with this situation. Again, he refused. I immediately fetched security, who removed the man from the building, and then set about comforting my colleague – who was quite distressed by the incident.

I believe that my resilience here, and refusal to cooperate with someone who displayed discriminatory behaviour, was the right call. We should never accept such behaviour, in any form.

Q2. In 200 words or less, tell us when you have demonstrated a positive drive.

Sample Response

For one of the modules on my university course, we were required to do a group presentation. I was paired up with 4 people whom I had never met before. Immediately, I noticed that the vibe from the group was extremely negative. The other 4 members of the group were not confident about our chances of giving a good presentation, and didn't seem enthused by the subject.

I immediately acted to try and improve the mood of the group. I started by asking each member of the group about which parts they were most interested in, and then assigning roles based on this. I wanted every single person to be equally involved in the project. At all times I tried to keep things light-hearted and interesting, whilst ensuring everyone stayed focused on the task. I naturally took on the role of leader for this task. Whenever I noticed a member of the group feeling down or disinterested in part of the task, I took them to one side and tried to motivate and encourage them.

The end result was that we gave a very successful presentation, and achieved top marks, with everyone commenting that my leadership skills had helped them.

Q3. In 200 words or less, give an example of when you have demonstrated your professionalism.

Sample Response

Whilst working at a local homeless shelter, I was tasked with helping an ethnic woman choose clothes. During a visit to a clothes store, a group of youths entered the shop, and immediately began shouting racial abuse at the woman. The woman was very distressed and upset by this.

Taking action, I immediately placed myself between the youths and woman, and informed them that their behaviour would not be tolerated. I called the shop manager over, who asked the youths to leave the shop, before ringing the police. After they had left, we took the woman into a back room of the shop, made her a cup of coffee and comforted her until the police arrived.

I assured her that the police would be able to deal with the incident, and did everything I could to make her feel safe and respected.

Q4. In 200 words or less, tell us about a time when you have demonstrated good service delivery.

Sample Response

Whilst working at a sports retailer, we had an angry customer come in. The man was upset because he had bought a pair of trainers for his daughter's birthday. However, she had opened the box to discover that it contained just one trainer. Now, on his daughter's birthday, he had been forced to come back to the store to return the product. The man was extremely upset by this.

The first thing I did was to calm him down and reassure him that I would deal with his problem. I made him a cup of coffee and fetched the manager. I suggested to the manager that we should offer the man a full refund, along with a replacement for the shoe that was missing. My manager agreed, and we returned to the man with the proposed offer. He immediately calmed down, and left the shop with his new product, pleased with the resolution.

The next day I rang the man, to check that he was happy with the level of service he had received. He told me that he was, and that despite the issue, he would continue to shop at our store.

Declaration

Finally, at the bottom of the form, you'll be asked to sign a declaration that all of the information you have provided is factually correct and that you've been honest. The form will also give you an extra space, in which you can enter any extra information that you think the police should know about.

Police Constable Assessment Centre

If you successfully pass the verbal reasoning assessment, then you will be invited to attend the Police Constable assessment centre. All candidates for the Detective Constable Direct Entry programme must go through this assessment centre, before moving onto the next stage – which is the Detective Constable Assessment Centre.

The regular police assessment centre will test you on slightly different competencies to that of a Detective Constable, albeit these are still extremely important in the grand scheme of things – as they exemplify the behavioural expectations. As we've already mentioned, the competencies for regular police officers are as follows:

PUBLIC SERVICE

Demonstrates a real belief in public service, focusing on what matters to the public and will best serve their interests. Understands the expectations, changing needs and concerns of different communities, and strives to address them. Builds public confidence by talking with people in local communities to explore their viewpoints and break down barriers between them and the police. Understands the impact and benefits of policing for different communities, and identifies the best way to deliver services to them. Works in partnership with other agencies to deliver the best possible overall service to the public.

OPENNESS TO CHANGE

Positive about change, adapting rapidly to different ways of working and putting effort into making them work. Flexible and open to alternative approaches to solving problems. Finds better, more cost-effective ways to do things, making suggestions for change. Takes an innovative and creative approach to solving problems.

SERVICE DELIVERY

Understands the organisation's objectives and priorities, and how own work fits into these. Plans and organises tasks effectively, taking a structured and methodical approach to achieving outcomes. Manages multiple tasks effectively by thinking things through in advance, prioritising and managing time well. Focuses on the outcomes to be achieved, working quickly and accurately and seeking guidance when appropriate.

PROFESSIONALISM

Acts with integrity, in line with the values and ethical standards of the Police Service. Takes ownership for resolving problems, demonstrating courage and resilience in dealing with difficult and potentially volatile situations. Acts on own initiative to address issues, showing a strong work ethic and demonstrating extra effort when required. Upholds professional standards, acting honestly and ethically, and challenges unprofessional conduct or discriminatory behaviour. Asks for and acts on feedback, learning from experience and developing own professional skills and knowledge. Remains calm and professional under pressure, defusing conflict and being prepared to step forward and take control when required.

DECISION MAKING

Gathers, verifies and assesses all appropriate and available information to gain an accurate understanding of situations. Considers a range of possible options before making clear, timely, justifiable decisions. Reviews decisions in the light of new information and changing circumstances. Balances risks, costs and benefits, thinking about the wider impact of decisions. Exercises discretion and applies professional judgement, ensuring actions and decisions are proportionate and in the public interest.

WORKING WITH OTHERS

Works co-operatively with others to get things done, willingly giving help and support to colleagues. Is approachable, developing positive working relationships. Explains things well, focusing on the key points and talking to people using language they understand. Listens carefully and asks questions to clarify understanding, expressing own views positively and constructively. Persuades people by stressing the benefits of a particular approach, keeps them informed of progress and manages their expectations. Is courteous, polite and considerate, showing empathy and compassion. Deals with people as individuals and addresses their specific needs and concerns. Treats people with respect and dignity, dealing with them fairly and without prejudice regardless of their background or circumstances.

Throughout the assessment centre, you'll be tested on these competencies.

What To Bring With You

For the assessment centre you will be required to take a number of important documents with you to confirm your identification to the police. The forms of identification can vary but the more common types include:

- A full 10-year passport or TWO of the following:

- British Driving Licence;

- P45;

- Birth Certificate, issued within six weeks of birth;

- Cheque Book and Bank Card with three statements and proof of signature;

- Card containing a photograph of yourself;

- Proof of residence, e.g. Council Tax, Gas, Electricity, Water or Telephone Bill.

Make sure that you read the information given to you and take along the relevant documents as if you do not, then you won't be able to continue with the day. At the assessment centre you will be required to undertake a numerical ability test, a verbal ability test, written exercises, interactive/roleplay exercises and a competency based structured interview.

Now, let's have a look at each of these exercises.

Numerical Ability Test

In the numerical ability test they will ask you to answer multiple-choice questions which will measure your ability to use numbers in a rational way, correctly identifying logical relationships between numbers and, drawing conclusions and inference from them. The numerical ability test will last for 23 minutes and there are 21 questions in the test. The test will not assess simple numerical checking ability. You will be presented with a series of graphs and tables, each followed by several questions. You must choose the correct answer from a maximum of four possible answers, filling in the appropriate space on an answer sheet they will provide. The questions will require you to utilise the following numerical operations:

- Addition

- Subtraction

- Multiplication

- Division

- Averages (mean)

- Percentages

- Ratios

- Interpretation of numbers represented graphically

You will take the test in an exercise room along with the other candidates in your group. You can use a calculator for this test which will be provided for you at the assessment centre. You are not permitted to use your own calculator during this test. They will give you full instructions before you start the test.

To give you an insight into the types of questions you'll face, here's a few examples:

Sample Question

You leave your house at 10:05. You travel for half an hour at 50 mph. When you reach the motorway, the traffic forces you to drive at 15 mph for 12 minutes. After the traffic clears, you continue your journey at 50 mph and arrive at your destination at 11:25.

1. Approximately, how far do you travel in total?

A – 80 miles

B – 60 miles

C – 20 miles

D – 30 miles

2. How long does the third part of your journey take?

A – 38 minutes

B – 22 minutes

C – 50 minutes

D – 44 minutes

3. How long would you have been travelling for if you had not got stuck in traffic, assuming you remained at 50 mph for the whole journey?

A – 1 hour and 2 minutes

B – 1 hour and 5 minutes

C – 1 hour and 15 minutes

D – 1 hour and 12 minutes

Verbal Ability

In the verbal ability test they will ask you to answer multiple choice questions which will measure your ability to make sense of a situation when you are given specific written information about it. These questions will be highly similar to the questions from the test that you took before the assessment centre.

The verbal ability test will last for 30 minutes and there are 28 questions in the test. Again, you will take the test in an exercise room along with the other candidates in your group. The test is split into two sections as follows — Section A of this test has three possible answers where only ONE of which is correct, whereas Section B has four possible answers of which only ONE is correct.

In Section A they will give you a number of conclusions which you might come to. You must look at each conclusion and work out if:

A the conclusion is true given the situation described and the facts known about it;

B the conclusion is false given the situation described and the facts known about it;

Or

C it is impossible to say whether the conclusion is true or false given the situation described and the facts known about it.

In Section B they will give you four statements and you will be required to evaluate which ONE of the four statements is the best answer, given the information provided. Once you have made your decision you will then fill in the appropriate space on an answer sheet they provide. They will give you full instructions before you start the test.

Since we've already given you good practice of answering the first set of questions, here's a sample question from Section B of the test:

Read the following passage and the answer options following, before deciding which ONE answer option is true.

Sample Verbal Question: Section B

At 09.30 this morning Constable Aziz collected the CCTV footage from the Eight to Late Shop on Main Street. He started to review the CCTV footage of the robbery at 14.30 that afternoon. While watching the footage he observed two men, wearing hooded tops (one grey and one green), enter the shop through the door at the back. The time recorded on the footage was 22.45. The men stood at the back of the shop, with only their backs in the view of the CCTV camera. There were four other people in the shop, three customers and a female sales assistant, at the time. The customers were a man and two women.

At 22.47 the two female customers, who appeared to be together, left the shop after paying for three bags of crisps. The other customer paid for a bottle of red wine and left the shop at 22.51. At 22.52 the man in the grey hooded top approached the sales assistant, who was behind the counter at the front of the shop, and appeared to speak to her. At this time the other man was standing near the entrance of the shop. After the exchange with the shop assistant the man took what appeared to be a handgun from his pocket and waved this in front of the sales assistant. The sales assistant appeared to open the till and then the man seemed to pass a bag over the counter.

At 22.56 the sales assistant started filling the bag. Constable Aziz then observed the shop door open and what appeared to be a man entering the shop. The man who had been standing at the back of the shop stepped forward and punched the man who had been entering the shop. The man who had thrown the punch then shouted at his friend, who then grabbed the bag from the sales assistant and both ran from the shop.

A. The shop was robbed by two men in hoodies in the early hours of the morning.

B. Two men in hoodies were seen by all three people in the shop.

C. CCTV footage shows two men in hoodies committing robbery in the shop with four witnesses.

D. The shop was robbed by two men, both wearing hoodies.

Sample Numerical Answer

Answers

1. B = 60 miles

2. A = 38 minutes

3. D = 1 hour and 12 minutes

Sample Verbal Answer

Answer = D

THE WRITTEN EXERCISES – REPORT WRITING

During the assessment centre you will be asked to take two written exercises. These will require you to create an Incident Report Form, based on the information given during the exercise. The following is an overview of the two exercises that you will have to carry out:

Written Exercise One. In this exercise, you will need to deal with a customer. The customer will be writing in to complain about how an incident was dealt with by your centre's security guard. You will be given 7 different sheets of paper, each containing a different take (from different witnesses) on the incident. Normally one of these will be from the security guard, detailing his view. You may or may not also be given CCTV based evidence (in written form) to look over. All 7 witness reports will differ, and therefore there will be discrepancies.

Your job is to write down the facts of the case, and at the end, make a recommendation about what should be done. Written Exercise Two. In this exercise, you will watch a 12 minute DVD of an interview between a witness to an incident at a shopping centre, and the security staff working at the centre. You will allowed to take notes during the screening, but there will be no pauses or breaks, and therefore you will need to take down as much important information as possible whilst watching the DVD. Your job is to take down all of the facts, and construct this into an incident report form, all whilst watching the DVD.

When you create a written report, the assessor is looking for a well-structured piece of writing that is logical and relevant.

You should demonstrate a good use and understanding of grammar, and aim to make zero spelling or grammatical errors. This is extremely important. You also need to make sure that your handwriting is neat and tidy, as this could reflect badly with your assessors.

The biggest factor in passing or failing this assessment, is your attention to detail. You cannot afford to miss key pieces of evidence or facts of the case, as you will be penalised for this. A great way to practice for the first exercise in particular is to look at a magazine or newspaper which reports on a particular event. Take a pen and paper, look through the story and then try to write down the key facts about the case.

The written report is an area of the police officer assessment process that many people do not think they need to practice. They use their preparation time before their assessment date predominantly looking at the role plays and the interview. The written report can actually gain you the highest percentage of marks out of all the assessment tests. This could mean the difference between a pass and a fail.

VISUAL EXERCISE

The second half of this exercise will be more challenging, and will require you to recognise visual evidence. You will be shown a DVD of an interview between a witness to an incident, and a shop assistant/ employee of an affected organisation, and will then be required to create an Incident Report Form based on what was said in the video.

Where the first exercise will challenge you on what it was you read, now you will be challenged on your ability to listen. Similarly to the first task, you need to be able to distinguish relevant information from irrelevant, and construct a well written report. The purpose of this exercise is for the assessors to determine whether you are someone who can work accurately under pressure, who will not allow any preconceived judgements or opinions to get in the way of good police work.

Here are some things to look out for during the visual exercise:

-   Pay close attention to what the person being interviewed is saying. You will not be given a second watch of the DVD, and therefore you need to glean as much detail from the first watch as possible.

- Watch out for any discrepancies or contradictions. Remember that not all witnesses are reliable, sometimes the witness may contradict themselves. In your report form, you will be given a space for further notes, where you can mention this; however the main body of the report form should only consist of facts.

- Remember that not every witness will be clear in what they are saying. People speak in a variety of different ways, and come from a variety of different backgrounds. You need to try as hard as possible to understand everyone who is being interviewed. At times, the interviewer in the DVD should make this easier for you by clarifying certain things.

- This exercise will test your perception of individuals. Remember that police officers are unbiased and never discriminatory. You should treat every single person that you meet in a fair and positive manner.

- Remember that the aim of this exercise isn't to find out whether someone is lying, it's to find out the truth. The people being interviewed aren't suspects, they are witnesses.

Role Play

During the police officer assessment centre you will have to deal with four interactive exercises or role plays as they are otherwise called. The type of situation that you will be confronted with varies greatly. However, examples of the types of exercises that have been used in the past include the following:

- A customer of the centre wants to discuss an incident that happened at the centre.

- A shop owner in the centre wants to discuss an incident at their shop.

- An employee within the centre has been asked to attend a meeting.

- A school teacher who is visiting the centre would like to discuss an issue with you regarding his/her pupils.

The situation that you will have to deal with is irrelevant. It is how you interact with the role play actor and what you say that is important. You must be able to demonstrate the police officer core competencies during each role play scenario.

Examples of how you would achieve this include:

- Dealing with the role play actor in a sensitive and supportive manner;

- Having respect for people's views and feelings;

- Seeing issues from others' points of view;

- Ask relevant questions to clarify the situation;

- Listening to people's needs and interests;

- Respecting confidentiality where appropriate;

- Presenting an appropriate image;

- Trying to sort out customers' problems as soon as possible;

- Make reference to any supporting documentation, policies or procedures;

- Confirming that the customer is happy with your offered solution.

- Keeping customers updated on any progress that you make.

It is crucial that you learn the core competencies and are also able to demonstrate them during each exercise.

This part of the selection process will be split into two five-minute parts. The first part will consist of the preparation phase and the second part will be the actual activity phase that you'll be assessed against.

In our fantastic book on how to pass the Police Officer Selection Process, we'll provide you with an in-depth sample role play exercises, plus huge amounts of sample questions and answers from all of the other exercises.

Assessment Centre Interview

As part of the police officer assessment centre you will normally be required to sit an interview that is based around the core competencies. Under normal circumstances the interview board will consist of two or three people. These can be from either the uniformed side of the service or support staff.

It is important to remember that whilst you will be nervous you should try not to let this get in the way of your success. Police officers, in general, are confident people who have the ability to rise to a challenge and perform under difficult and pressurised situations. Treat the interview no differently to this. You ARE capable of becoming a police officer and the nerves that you have on the day are only natural, in fact they will help you to perform better if you have prepared sufficiently. The crucial element to your success, as with the rest of the selection process, is your preparation.

The police interview board will have a number of set questions to choose from and, whilst these are constantly changing, they will usually form part of the police officer core competencies.

Before attending your interview ensure that you read, digest and understand the police core competencies. Without these it will be difficult to pass the interview.

The interview will last for up to 20 minutes and will ask you four questions about how you have dealt with specific situations in the past. These questions will be related to the competency areas relevant to the role of a police officer, which we have shown you earlier in this guide.

They will give you up to five minutes to answer each question. The person interviewing you will stop you if you go over the five minutes. As the person interviewing you asks you the question, they will also give you a written copy of the question to refer to. They may ask you further questions to help you to give a full response. When you consider your responses to the interview questions, you should only choose examples that you feel comfortable discussing with the person interviewing you.

The person who interviews you will assess your responses against the type of behaviours you need to perform effectively in the role. You must make sure that you are familiar with the competencies and that your answer gives you an opportunity to explain how you have shown this behaviour.

PREPARING FOR THE ASSESSMENT CENTRE INTERVIEW

When preparing for the assessment centre competency based interview you should try to formulate responses to questions that surround the assessable core competencies.

The responses that you provide should be specific examples of where you have been in that particular scenario. In your 'welcome pack', which will be sent to you approximately 2 weeks before the date of your assessment centre, you should find examples of the 'core competencies' relevant to a police officer. These are the criteria that you will be scored against so it is worthwhile reading them beforehand and trying to structure your answers around them as best you can. For example, one of the sections you will be assessed against could be 'Working with Others'. You may be asked a question where you have to give an example of where you worked effectively as part of a team in order to achieve a difficult task or goal. Try to think of an example where you have had to do this and structure your answer around the core competencies required, e.g. you worked cooperatively with the others, supported the rest of the team members and persuaded them to follow your ideas for completing the task.

Below we've provided you with a sample question and response, based around the core competency of professionalism.

Question – Please provide an example of where you have taken responsibility to resolve a problem?

"After reading an appeal in my local paper from a local charity I decided to try to raise money for this worthwhile cause by organising a charity car wash day at the local school during the summer holidays. I decided that the event would take place in a month's time, which would give me enough time to organise such an event. The head teacher at the school agreed to support me during the organisation of the event and provide me with the necessary resources required to make it a success.

I set about organising the event and soon realised that I had made a mistake in trying to arrange everything on my own, so I arranged for two of my work colleagues to assist me. Once they had agreed to help me I started out by providing them with a brief of what I wanted them to do. I informed them that, in order for the event to be a success, we needed to act with integrity and professionalism at all times. I then asked one of them to organise the booking of the school and arrange local sponsorship in the form of buckets, sponges and car wash soap to use on the day, so that we did not have to use our own personal money to buy them. I asked the second person to arrange advertising in the local newspaper and radio stations so that we could let the local community know about our charity car wash event, which would in turn hopefully bring in more money on the day for the charity.

Following a successful advertising campaign, I was inundated with calls from local newspapers about our event and it was becoming hard work having to keep talking to them and explaining what the event was all about. But I knew that this information was important if we were to raise our target of £500.

Everything was going well right up to the morning of the event, when I realised we had not got the key to open the school gates. It was the summer holidays so the caretaker was not there to open the gates for us. Not wanting to let everyone down, I jumped in my car and made my way down to the caretaker's house and managed to wake him up and get the key just in time before the car wash event was due to start. In the end the day was a great success and we all managed to raise £600 for the local charity. Throughout the event I put in lots of extra effort in order to make it a great success.

Once the event was over I decided to ask the head teacher for feedback on how he thought I had managed the project. He provided me with some excellent feedback and some good pointers for how I might improve in the future when organising events. I took on-board his feedback in order to improve my skills."

Verbal Reasoning Test

Following the police constable assessment day, you'll be asked to complete an online verbal reasoning assessment. The verbal reasoning assessment will challenge you on your ability to answer a question based on a passage. You'll need to read the whole passage, and then will be given one statement. There are 30 passages, and 30 questions, with one question per passage. After each statement will be the words TRUE, FALSE and IMPOSSIBLE TO SAY. Your task is to decide which category each statement falls under.

When answering the questions, you must only answer based on information provided in the passage. So, if you get a statement that reads, 'It was raining on Tuesday 17th April', and the passage also says that it was raining on the 17th April, you must select true – even if this wasn't the case in real life.

Here's a breakdown of how to decide on each answer:

TRUE. You should answer with TRUE only if the passage definitively states that this is the case. Do not make assumptions, and do not use information from the real world, when answering.

FALSE. You should only answer with FALSE if the passage definitively states that this is not the case, or disproves the statement. For example, if the passage states that 'the car involved in the accident was black', but the question states 'The car involved in the accident was brown', then the answer is false. Do not make assumptions, and do not use information from the real world, when answering.

IMPOSSIBLE TO SAY. You should only answer with IMPOSSIBLE TO SAY if the passage does not give a clear answer. For example, if the question states that 'the robber named Matthew was arrested', but the passage states that 'two of the three robbers were arrested', then you cannot definitively say that Matthew was one of these – and therefore the answer is IMPOSSIBLE TO SAY.

Verbal reasoning tests your attention to detail, and your ability to work efficiently when dealing with written information. With this in mind, it's imperative that you conduct in-depth preparation BEFORE you sit the test. Start preparing for this assessment before you even fill in the application form. Don't get into the test and try to wing it, because this won't work. Given the opportunity available, there is simply no excuse not to conduct as much prep work as possible.

Below we've provided you with a sample verbal reasoning question, along with a breakdown of how to go about answering it.

Sample Verbal Reasoning Question

Carefully read through the passage below. Answer the questions following the passage with TRUE, FALSE or IMPOSSIBLE TO SAY. Circle the correct answer.

The Office for National Statistics said internet shopping and sales of household goods had been better in October compared with previous months. However, sales of clothing and footwear, where many retailers cut prices before Christmas, were particularly weak.

The increase came as a surprise to many analysts who were predicting a 0.4% fall in internet shopping and sales of household goods. The rise meant that retail sales volumes in the three months to January were up by 2.6% on the previous quarter. The final quarter of the year is a better guide to the underlying trend than one month's figures.

Some analysts cautioned that the heavy seasonal adjustment of the raw spending figures at the turn of the year made interpreting the data difficult. Even so, the government will be relieved that spending appears to be holding up despite the squeeze on incomes caused by high inflation, rising unemployment, a weak housing market and the crisis in the eurozone.

Retail sales account for less than half of total consumer spending and do not include the purchase of cars or eating out. The ONS said that its measure of inflation in the high street – the annual retail sales deflator – fell to 2.2% last month, its lowest level since November 2009. Ministers are hoping that lower inflation will boost real income growth during the course of 2012.

Q1. Ministers hope that higher inflation will boost real income growth during 2012.

True   **False**   **Impossible to Say**

Answer

Q1. FALSE

The reason that this answer is false, is because the passage clearly states that, 'Ministers are hoping that lower inflation will boost real income growth during the course of 2012.' You will notice that they use the word lower here, and not higher.

Now that you've seen how to go about answering one of these questions, have a go at some sample verbal reasoning questions. After the test, we've provided you with all the answers, so have a look and see how you get on.

Verbal Reasoning Test

Employees who attain fifteen years' continuous service between 7th November 2003 and 30th June 2007 shall qualify for the long-service payment at the rate applicable at the time. Employees who are promoted to a higher role during this period will cease to qualify for the payment but will receive a minimum pay increase on promotion of £300 per annum, which will be achieved through partial protection of the long-service payment.

Where the pay assimilation process on 7th November 2003 created a basic pay increase of more than 7%, and the employee was in receipt of the long-service payment, the payment has been reduced with effect from that date by the amount that the increase exceeded 7%. The consequent pay rates were set out in circular NJC/01/04. Pay protection for employees on the retained duty system

Where an employee on the retained duty system has not received a pay increase of at least 7% (for the same pattern and level of activity) following full implementation of the pay award effective from 7th November 2003, the fire and rescue authority may introduce arrangements to ensure that such an increase is achieved.

The NJC recognises that in the early stages of implementing the Integrated Personal Development System it may, on occasions, be difficult to apply the principles at Paragraph 19 of Section 4 Part B. Fire and rescue authorities, employees and trade unions should therefore adopt a co-operative and common-sense approach to any problems that might arise.

Q1. If an employee who is on the retained duty system has not received a pay increase of at least 7% following the introduction of the pay award, the fire and rescue service must introduce arrangements to ensure that such an increase is achieved.

True   **False**   **Impossible to Say**

A data warehouse is the main source of information for an organisation's historical data. Its historical data is often referred to as its corporate memory. As an example of how a data warehouse can be put to good use, an organisation would use the information stored in its data warehouse to find out how many particular stock items they sold on a particular day in a particular year. They could also ascertain which employees were off sick on any given day or any given year. The data stored within the warehouse contains essential information so that managers can make appropriate management decisions.

A data warehouse is normally large in size as the information stored usually focuses on basic, structured and organised data. Some of the characteristics of the data in a data warehouse are as follows:

Time-variant - changes to the data in the database are tracked and recorded so that reports can be produced showing changes over time;

Non-volatile - the data in the database is never over-written or deleted but is retained for future reporting;

Integrated - the database contains data from most or all of an organisation's operational applications and this data is useful and meaningful for further processing and analysis.

Q2. Integrated and non-volatile data form some of the characteristics of a data warehouse.

True   **False**   **Impossible to Say**

You must protect the safety and health of everyone in your workplace, including people with disabilities, and provide welfare facilities for your employees.

Basic things you need to consider are outlined below.

Welfare facilities

For your employees' well-being you need to provide:

- toilets and hand basins, with soap and towels or a handdryer;
- drinking water;
- a place to store clothing (and somewhere to change if special clothing is worn for work);
- somewhere to rest and eat meals.

Health issues

To have a healthy working environment, make sure there is:

- good ventilation – a supply of fresh, clean air drawn from outside or a ventilation system;
- a reasonable working temperature (usually at least 16°C, or 13°C for strenuous work, unless other laws require lower temperatures);
- lighting suitable for the work being carried out;
- enough room space and suitable workstations and seating;
- a clean workplace with appropriate waste containers.

Safety issues

To keep your workplace safe, you must:

- properly maintain your premises and work equipment;
- keep floors and traffic routes free from obstruction;
- have windows that can be opened and also cleaned safely;
- make sure that any transparent (eg glass) doors or walls are protected or made of safety material.

Q3. It is the responsibility of the employee for keeping a workplace safe.

True   **False**   **Impossible to Say**

The entire selection process for becoming a magistrate can take approximately 12 months, sometimes longer depending on the area.

Once you have been accepted you will be required to undertake a comprehensive training course which is usually held over a 3-day period (18 hours). During this course you will learn the necessary skills that are required in order to become a magistrate.

The training is normally carried out by the Justice Clerk who is responsible for the court. He/she will usually be the legal advisor during your magistrate sittings. They will help you to develop all the necessary skills required in order to carry out your duties professionally and competently.

You will carry out your training as part of a group with other people who have been recruited at the same time as you. This is extremely beneficial as it will allow you to learn in a safe environment.

Training will be given using a variety of methods, which may include pre-course reading, small-group work, use of case studies, computer-based training and CCTV. It is recognised that magistrates are volunteers and that their time is valuable, so every effort is made to provide all training at times and places convenient to trainees. The Ministry of Justice booklet 'Serving as a Magistrate' has more information about the magistracy and the role of magistrates.

Q4. The comprehensive training course for becoming a magistrate usually consists of 3 days which is divided into 6 hours training per day.

True   False   Impossible to Say

People pay National Insurance contributions in order to build up their entitlement to a state pension and other social security benefits.

The amount that you pay is directly linked to the amount you earn. If you earn over a certain amount, your employer deducts Class 1 National Insurance contributions from your wages through the PAYE system.

You pay a lower rate of National Insurance contributions if you're a member of your employer's 'contracted-out' pension scheme, or you're a married woman – or widow – who holds a valid 'election certificate'.

Your employer also pays employer National Insurance contributions based on your earnings and on any benefits you get with your job, for example a company car. HMRC keeps track of your contributions through your National Insurance number. This is like an account number and is unique to you.

Q5. People pay National Insurance contributions in order to build up housing benefits.

True   **False**   **Impossible to Say**

Janet and Steve have been married for twenty-seven years. They have a daughter called Jessica who is twenty-five-years-old. They all want to go on holiday together but cannot make up their minds on where to go.

Janet's first choice would be somewhere hot and sunny abroad. Her second choice would be somewhere in their home country that involves a sporting activity. She does not like hill-climbing or walking holidays but her third choice would be a skiing holiday.

Steve's first choice would be a walking holiday in the hills somewhere in their home country and his second choice would be a sunny holiday abroad. He does not enjoy skiing. Jessica's first choice would be a skiing holiday and her second choice would be a sunny holiday abroad. Jessica's third choice would be a walking holiday in the hills of their home country.

Q6. Jessica's first choice would be a walking holiday in the hills of their home country.

True   **False**   **Impossible to Say**

The Special Air Service was originally founded by Lieutenant David Stirling during World War II. The initial purpose of the regiment was to be a long-range desert patrol group required to conduct raids and sabotage operations far behind enemy lines.

Lieutenant Stirling was a member of Number 8 Commando Regiment and he specifically looked for recruits who were both talented and individual specialists in their field, and who also had initiative.

The first mission of the SAS turned out to be a disaster. They were operating in support of Field Marshal Claude Auchinleck's attack in November 1941, but only 22 out of 62 SAS troopers deployed reached the rendezvous point. However, Stirling still managed to organise another attack against the German airfields at Aqedabia, Site and Agheila, which successfully destroyed 61 enemy aircraft without a single casualty. After that, the 1st SAS earned regimental status and Stirling's brother Bill began to arrange a second regiment called Number 2 SAS.

It was during the desert war that they performed a number of successful insertion missions and destroyed many aircraft and fuel depots in the process. Their success contributed towards Hitler issuing his Kommandobefehl order to execute all captured Commandos. The Germans then stepped up security and as a result the SAS changed their tactics. They used jeeps armed with Vickers K machine guns and used tracer ammunition to ignite fuel and aircraft. When the Italians captured David Stirling, he ended up in Colditz Castle as a prisoner of war for the remainder of the war. His brother, Bill Stirling, and 'Paddy' Blair Mayne, then took command of the regiment.

Q7. During the SAS's first mission only 42 of the total troopers deployed reached the rendezvous point.

True   **False**   **Impossible to Say**

Applicants who successfully complete the online assessment, the physical aptitude test and the interview will be invited to attend a medical assessment. Applicants must satisfy all medical requirements in order to progress to the next stage. Details of the medical are as follows:

HEALTH QUESTIONNAIRE

Applicants will be required to accurately answer questions regarding their medical history.

PHYSICAL EXAMINATION

Applicants will be required to successfully pass a medical examination by the Medical Officer. This includes, amongst others, the following five elements:

• Lung function test.

• Hearing test.

• Vision test (including colour vision).

• Urine test.

• Pathology test.

TIME

The entire employment medical assessment will take approximately 1½ hours to complete.

Q8. There are 5 different elements to the medical.

True   False   Impossible to Say

There are two different types of bushfires in Australia - grass fires and forest fires. Grass fires more commonly occur on grazing and farm land. These often destroy fences, livestock, machinery, and they sometimes claim lives. Forest fires are largely made up of eucalyptus trees. These are extremely difficult to control due to the high amounts of flammable vapour from the leaves. The bushfires are fought by large numbers of trained volunteer fire-fighters. Helicopters and light aircraft are sometimes used to make observations about the fire and some also have the capacity to carry water. Aircraft used to carry water in order to extinguish forest fires often find that the visibility is extremely poor. This prevents them from getting close enough to the fire in order to extinguish it with their quantities of water.

Aircraft are used to make observations about the fire. This includes:

• Establishing which direction the fire is travelling;

• Locating suitable grid references to make fire-breaks to prevent firespread;

• Locating nearby homes, businesses, other buildings and livestock that are in danger from the fire spreading.

Q9. Aircraft deployed to extinguish bushfires struggle to get close to the fire due to the poor visibility.

True   **False**   **Impossible to Say**

The time is 6:37pm on Sunday the 7th of February 2010. A two-car diesel multiple unit, which has been travelling on the west Highland Line in Scotland heading towards Aviemore, has derailed and caught fire as a result. One carriage has been left in a precarious position on the 40-foot high embankment whilst the remaining three carriages have come to rest blocking both the upside and downside tracks. In addition to blocking the lines, the incident has also caused the closure of the A35 road which is located directly below the rail line.

The train involved in the incident is a First ScotRail Class 120 Turbostar unit 156TGE. The driver of the train is a 52-year-old male named as George McDermott and the train's headcode is 6Y56. Witnesses claim that the train derailed after hitting a large boulder which had come to rest on the track following a landslide. In total, there are 34 passengers on the four carriage train. There are a number of casualties. Amongst others, an elderly female who is 72-year-old is suffering from a suspected broken collar-bone; a 32-year-old male is suffering from a serious head injury and a 21-year-old pregnant female is suffering from shock and a broken finger. The Rail Control Centre has informed all oncoming trains of the incident and has operated red stop signals along the route.

The weather is severely hampering rescue operations and the Fire and Rescue Commander has indicated that there could be a significant delay before all casualties are safely removed from the scene. The local weather centre has forecast gales of up to 60 miles per hour over the next 12 hours with temperatures dropping to minus 3 degrees.

Q10. The current temperature is minus 3 degrees.

True   **False**   **Impossible to Say**

Answers

Q1. False

Q2. True

Q3. Impossible to Say

Q4. Impossible to Say

Q5. Impossible to Say

Q6. False

Q7. False

Q8. False

Q9. True

Q10. False

FOR MORE HELP WITH PASSING THE POLICE CONSTABLE ASSESSMENT CENTRE CHECK OUT OUR VERBAL REASONING TESTS WORKBOOK!

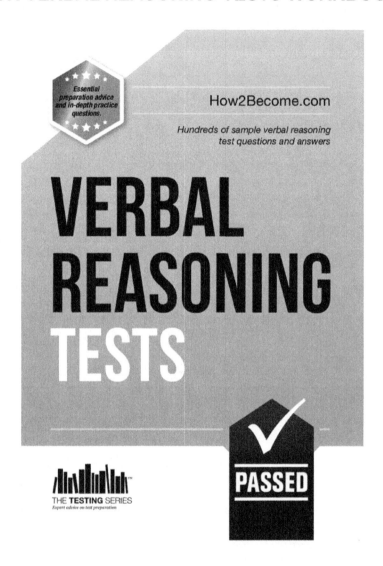

FOR MORE CAREER ADVICE GO TO:
WWW.HOW2BECOME.COM

Detective Assessment Centre: Day 1

If you manage to pass the Police Constable Assessment Centre then you will be invited to attend a Detective Constable Assessment Centre. There are two stages to this assessment centre: Day 1 and Day 2. In this chapter, we will provide you with all of the information that you need in order to pass the Detective Constable Day 1.

During the assessment centre, you will be required to take 3 exercises. These exercises are as follows:

-    An In-tray exercise

-    A briefing exercise

-    An interview

All of the exercises have been created with the Detective Constable role in mind. Both the In-tray and the briefing will place you in the role of a qualified Detective Constable. Following the completion of each exercise, you will be required to fill in a 'self-reflection' form. This is essentially a form which gives you the opportunity to note down what you think you did well during the exercise, and what you think you could have done better. The self-reflection forms are an important part of the assessment, and the police will look at these when assessing your overall performance.

The core competencies will play a crucial role in how well you score at the assessment centre. In every single exercise, you should be aiming to demonstrate that you have these competencies and understand why they are important to the role. Before you attend the assessment centre, make sure you sit down and study the competencies in careful detail. If you cannot show an in-depth understanding of the competencies then you will not pass the assessment centre and progress to the next stage.

Now, let's look at the exercises in detail.

In-Tray Exercise

In-Tray is a paper-based exercise which simulates an office environment. The goal of the exercise is to be similar to a normal working day for the job which you are applying for. Therefore, In-Tray is an excellent way to measure a candidate's ability and see whether they work in a way which is conducive to the job and business as a whole.

In a sense, the In-Tray exercise is like a role play exercise. You are asked to assume a role, then, under the specification given, you are expected to complete the tasks presented to you. Generally speaking, this involves being given a collection of tasks to complete: your job is not only to complete these tasks, but to also prioritise them in an order which means you're most likely to complete them all in time.

Different pieces of work will have varying deadlines. Likewise, you might find a piece of work later in your assessment which has a tighter deadline. Therefore, it might be the case that this newer piece of work needs to take precedence over everything else, which can be put to one side for the time being.

The Detective Constable assessment centre takes a slightly different approach than you would normally expect. Instead of prioritising the issues in order, you will need to write a report, based on what you've read – summarising your main priorities, how you would order the issues, and what actions you will take based on this.

During the In-Tray exercise, you will be tested on the following competencies:

- Emotional Awareness

- Communication

- Professional Approach

- Investigative Mind

- Learning

Below we've listed a brief example, to give you an idea of what we mean:

Example In-Tray Question

Here you are a new member of staff, replying to a letter of complaint from a customer regarding a faulty product. The customer's letter of complaint contains photos of the faulty product. For the sake of this example, let's assume that the background information for the exercise states that customers can receive a full refund if the product is either faulty or has not been opened. Your options are as follows:

Option 1. Reply to the letter offering a full refund for the faulty product, whilst also apologising for the time it has cost the customer.

Option 2. Reply to the letter stating that, since the customer has opened the packaging of the product, they cannot receive a refund. Apologise for the inconvenience.

Option 3. Forward the letter to your manager, who can assess whether or not the product is faulty.

Option 4. Ignore the letter since the customer cannot receive a refund.

How To Prioritise

When looking at the above options, you need to think logically. Firstly, the customer has complained that their product is faulty, and has provided evidence for this. Therefore, you can assume that it is faulty. Following from this, you can read the background information which contains the company's policy regarding refunds. Since the product is faulty, the customer is allowed a refund. Therefore, the second and fourth answer options are inappropriate.

This leaves you with the first and third options. How you answer will depend on the information given to you during the exercise. For example, if you have a calendar which shows that your manager is busy throughout the day, then it would not be wise to forward it to them. Likewise, if your job description gives you clearance to issue refunds, then the first option is most suitable.

Writing Your Report

So, you've prioritised the options – now you need to put them in the form of a written report. When it comes to the Detective Constable In-tray exercises, the police won't actually expect you to write the report in the way that a real Detective Constable would, using knowledge of CID protocol and crime scene evidence. However, what they will expect is for you to put together a logical and grammatically correct response, which accurately prioritises the issues and provides good justification for why you've done so. It's extremely important to pay close attention to the grammatical elements of your report, and this will also be really important in the briefing exercise. Below we've given you an example response to the above customer complaint exercise. Let's assume that in this case, you were writing the letter in response to a senior colleague.

Dear Mr Ramsden,

When evaluating the options that were presented to me, the first thing I did was to weigh out the customer's claims against the company policy. Our company policy clearly states that if a product is faulty, then they shall be granted a refund. For this reason, both options two and four are incorrect.

Following this, I then needed to decide on the best course of action. As a new member of staff, I felt that I was not in a position to decide on whether a product was faulty, and that this was something which could best be decided by the manager of the store. With this in mind, I passed the letter on to my senior, along with the details. Although I am always happy to take responsibility, I felt that an issue such as this could be better handled by a senior manager, who has a more in-depth level of product knowledge than me.

Sincerely,

Jessica.

Hopefully the above gives you some idea of how to construct your response. The above response is really short, as it's a small exercise with only a few options. Naturally, you can expect the assessment centre exercise to be more in-depth. You'll be given a lot more options, and therefore will have much more to write about.

Below we have provided you with two sample In-Tray exercises. The first of these is not police-based, but it should give you good practice towards making decisions and prioritising issues. Our exercise will help you to think logically and pragmatically about difficult and complex situations. For the purposes of this exercise, you will be asked to prioritise **as you go.**

In the second exercise, we have given you a mock-up of the real thing – with police based issues. At the end of this test you will need to make a **final written report**, which is the same as at the Detective Constable assessment centre.

Sample In-Tray Exercise 1

Part 1: Background Information

The British Government has recently created new voting laws, bringing younger people into the fold as they are now allowed to vote. The new voting law states that those who are at least sixteen years old are eligible to vote in local, general, and special elections. Moreover, six-teen-year-olds will be eligible to vote in any upcoming referendums.

With the legal voting age lowering from eighteen to sixteen, the country is preparing for an added 1.6 million sixteen and seventeen-year-olds being eligible to vote. While it's not likely that all of these 1.6 million people will vote, they will still need to be added to the electoral roll and register.

Another change made to British electoral roll was a change from an opt-in 'register to vote' system to an opt-out model. This means that, on an individual's sixteenth birthday, they will automatically be added to the electoral roll. In the outgoing system, the public had to register to vote, essentially opting in to the electoral roll. Now, the public will need to opt out. The goal of this was to reduce the number of barriers between the general public and voting, in order to make the UK more democratic.

This presents a significant task to the UK Civil Service. Not only do 1.6 million new sixteen and seventeen-year-old voters need to be added to the electoral roll, but anyone else in the UK who was previously not registered will now automatically be added. Of the approximate 45 million who are eligible to vote in the UK, roughly a third of them were not registered to vote in the 2017 general election. This means that approximately 15 million people will need to be added to the electoral roll.

The result of this initiative means that people will no longer have to register to vote – they will already be registered. However, those who wish to vote by postal or proxy will still need to apply as normal.

Rather than manually handling data for over 15 million people, the Civil Service has decided that software will be used to automatically enrol the currently unregistered members of the public. This means that a piece of software must be decided on.

Your Role

As a member of the Civil Service, you will be part of the initiative to bring voters onto the electoral roll. You will be working as part of a team which is devoted to this task. As the leader of this team, you will be in charge of co-ordinating the rest of the members to create an efficient way of automatically adding all of the eligible general public to the electoral roll.

You've been working for the Civil Service for some time and have led smaller projects before. However, this is the first project of this scale in which you've been placed in charge of a big team.

During the project, your duties will include:

1. Co-ordinating with your entire team so that the project can be completed by the deadline.

2. Collating information on any issues that your team is facing, either resolving them yourself or handing them to staff who can.

3. Liaising with members of other teams in order to enhance co-operation and productivity.

4. Meeting with managers regularly to keep them updated on progress.

5. Assisting in data handling and software management.

6. Deciding on a suitable piece of software to handle the data handling process.

Your Team

The relevant team members for this exercise are:

- James Williams, a member of the Civil Service for 3 years. He is experienced in data handling, and has been involved in projects of a similar size in the past. James works full-time.

- Lily Kemp, a member of the Civil Service for 1 year. Lily joined the Civil Service as part of a graduate scheme, and has shown to be talented when it comes to troubleshooting issues with software. While she has no professional experience in IT, Lily shows an incredible aptitude for computers in her hobbies.

There are a further ten team members that you will also be leading.

Other Personnel

As well as your team, you should also be aware of the following:

- Cynthia Johnson, your manager. She is overseeing the entire project, which means that you will need to report any issues directly to her. Cynthia works full-time, but is often busy in meetings. This means that she might not be immediately available.

- Megan McColl, your contact from the IT department. Megan has offered to consult your team if any IT-related issues arise. Megan works full-time.

WE ADVISE THAT YOU TAKE SOME NOTES BEFORE
PROCEEDING TO THE NEXT STAGE:

Sample In-Tray Exercise, Part 2: Prioritising Tasks

Document 1 – Printed Email with Attachments

To: you@civilservice.com

Subject: Possible software solutions

----,

Thank you for taking on this project. We appreciate that this will be a significant undertaking for yourself, as well as all of us. However, we believe that we have chosen the right individual to oversee the handling of data to prepare the country for these major changes to the electoral system. This is an exciting opportunity to serve the UK population, since they voted for a party who decided that lowering the voting age is the correct thing to do. Therefore, it's our duty to ensure that this is carried out as thoroughly as possible.

As previously mentioned, you and your team are being tasked with handling and transferring data for over 15 million UK citizens. This is a huge undertaking. Thankfully, you won't be doing this by hand. We will be using software and other tools to speed up the process.

This brings me to your first task: deciding on the software that we will be using for this project. We have gathered a list of four different suites which we believe may be useful for the project. We would like you to decide on the best piece of software depending on the following criteria:

Cost. The budget for this software is £300,000, so we've already narrowed down the list. You must pick the software which you believe will provide the best value for money.

Transfer rate. Since there are 16 million documents to transfer, we need a piece of software which can transfer data as quickly as possible.

Error rate. We would prefer this entire system to be automated since it will save time. However, machines can be prone to error. Choose a piece of software with the lowest error-rate possible.

Data protection facilities. Data protection is a key part of our role here in the Civil Service. We must ensure that all data uploaded and transferred by this software is secure and in line with the Data Protection Act.

You will also be required to read our Data Protection Policy, which includes the Data Protection Act, before we proceed with this project. This will be sent to you later today. Please confirm that you have read the document within thirty minutes of it being sent to you, so that we can continue.

Thanks,

Cynthia.

Attachment 1

Software Name: Runsfer.

Cost: £250,000.

Transfer Rate: 3 seconds per document, per machine (up to fifteen machines).

Error Rate: 1 per 100,000 documents.

Data Protection Facilities: Encryption, login authentication.

Attachment 2

Software Name: Dart Transfer.

Cost: £280,000.

Transfer Rate: 2.5 seconds per document, per machine (unlimited machines).

Error Rate: 2 per 100,000 documents.

Data Protection Facilities: Encryption, login authentication, VPN (Virtual Private Network) firewalls.

Attachment 3
Software Name: Library Ladder Transfer Solution
Cost: £200,000.
Transfer Rate: 4 seconds per document, per machine (up to ten machines).
Error Rate: 0.5 per 100,000 documents.
Data Protection Facilities: Encryption.

Attachment 4
Software Name: Super Speed Transfer.
Cost: £299,999.
Transfer Rate: 2 seconds per document, per machine (unlimited machines).
Error Rate: 0.75 per 100,000 documents.
Data Protection Facilities: Encryption.

Task 1

Choose the **most effective** course of action:

Reply suggesting that 'Runsfer' be chosen as the data transfer software.	
Reply suggesting that 'Dart Transfer' be chosen as the data transfer software.	
Reply suggesting that 'Library Ladder Transfer Solution' be chosen as the data transfer software.	
Reply suggesting that 'Super Speed Transfer' be chosen as the data transfer software.	

Document 2 – Letter with Attached Personnel Document

----,

I'm just writing to let you know that we'll be adding another member to your team today. They had been assigned to another project recently, but thankfully the deadline was met incredibly easily, leaving them with room to move onto something new.

I've attached the candidate's details in the following document, giving you an idea of who they are, how they work, and what they're experienced in.

Please come to a decision about what role they will be fulfilling *before* they join your team at 11:30am today.

Thanks,

Nina,

Human Resources.

Attachment 1

Name: Oliver Reeves

Previous Department/Project: Drafting legislation for upcoming changes to the UK education system.

Talent Areas: PR, legislative writing, communications.

Development Areas: IT.

Working Style: Primarily independent, but also capable of team-working.

Task 2

Choose the **most effective** and **least effective** course of action:

	Most Effective	Least Effective
Assign Oliver IT tasks.		
Have Oliver act as a liaison between yourself and the rest of the team.		
Assign Oliver the task of writing a report explaining what the plan for the enrolment project is, writing regular updates for your manager to read.		
Place Oliver in a position so that he can work closely with Lily and develop his IT skills.		

Document 3 – Policy Document

DATA PROTECTION POLICY

Before continuing, it is vital that all team members on the Electoral Roll project read and agree to the organisation's data protection policy.

All staff are expected to read, understand, and implement policies and actions which are in line with the Data Protection Act (1998).

In particular, parts I, II, and III are expected to be understood by all staff before proceeding with any project that involves handling personal data. What constitutes 'personal data' is addressed in the Data Protection Act.

On top of the Data Protection Act, our data protection policy encompasses the following key points. Staff are expected to follow these at all times:

1. ***All personal data is confidential.*** *Staff are reminded not to discuss any personal data outside of a purely professional context with other authorised staff. Discussing the details of this data with anyone outside of the Civil Service **is strictly forbidden.***

2. ***Personal data must be stored securely.*** *Staff must not use their regular email to attach and send data. If you do need to share information, contact IT and have them give you access to encrypted email facilities. Screens are to remain locked when staff are not at their desk.*

3. ***Personal data must be disposed of securely.*** *Any printed pieces of data are to be sent to a shredding room to be disposed of as safely as possible. Data must not be thrown into regular bins after use.*

4. ***Personal data is not to leave the building.*** *While flexible-working is encouraged, data must not be taken out of this building. Likewise, data must not be sent to computers, laptops, mobile phones, or other devices which have not been fitted with essential security software.*

Finally, we would like to remind all staff that breaking these rules will result in disciplinary action.

Task 3

Choose the **most effective** course of action:

Read the data protection policy document before replying to Cynthia to confirm that you have read and understand the rules and guidelines.	
Reply to Cynthia, informing her that you have read and understand the rules and guidelines, before reading the data protection policy later in your own time.	
Read the data protection policy document, as well as the Data Protection Act, before replying to Cynthia to confirm that you have read and understand the rules and guidelines.	
Ignore the data protection policy document and continue with your work.	

Document 4 – Letter of Complaint

----,

It has come to my attention that a member of your team has been breaking the rules of our data protection policy. This member of your team was overheard discussing personal information for a number of UK citizens in one of the break rooms.

A member of my team was the one who noticed and overheard this breach in security policy. I hope that you will deal with this matter sensibly and in a way which sends a good message to staff regarding the vitally important issue of data protection.

Yours sincerely,

Carl Jackson

Public Relations

Task 4

Choose the **most effective** and **least effective** course of action:

	Most Effective	Least Effective
Reply to the letter, asking to meet with Carl, your team member, and his team member.		
Reply to the letter, asking Carl to give you the name of the team member who was breaking these rules. Meet with this team member privately and discuss the issue with them before taking it further.		
Contact your manager and ask her what she thinks you should do.		

Hold a meeting with your entire team asking the person who broke the rules to come forward.		

Document 5 – Letter

----,

As you were informed at the start of this project, I have been chosen to be your consultant in the IT department. I've been keeping an eye on how the data handling has proceeded so far, and the software you've chosen, and I've noticed a couple of potential problems that I'd like to run by you before the project begins.

Firstly, we need to make sure that we have enough machines that we can commit to the data transfer process. Preferably, these need to be more powerful computers - ordinary laptops are too prone to overheating and error in order to be reliable. Thankfully, the software you have chosen comes with licenses for unlimited machines, so we can use as many as we can get our hands on.

Secondly, we need to find a method for checking errors which emerge during the process. The software is likely to come across a few errors - approximately 300 in total. If I have access to the software, I might be able to set up an alert system. I'll be able to stay notified of any errors. Once these have been collected, I'll send them to your team so that the errors can be rectified.

Kind regards,

Megan McColl,

IT

Task 5

Choose the **most effective** and **least effective** course of action:

	Most Effective	Least Effective
Reply to Megan, asking for her to lend you some additional computers for the project.		
Ignore the email. There's no need for any correspondence at this time.		
Reply to Megan to confirm that you will contact her if any extra computers are needed. You also confirm that you will grant her access to the software once it has been purchased and installed.		
Ask Lily to reply to Megan's letter.		

Answers

Task 1

Choose the **most effective** course of action:

Reply suggesting that 'Runsfer' be chosen as the data transfer software.	
Reply suggesting that 'Dart Transfer' be chosen as the data transfer software.	✓
Reply suggesting that 'Library Ladder Transfer Solution' be chosen as the data transfer software.	
Reply suggesting that 'Super Speed Transfer' be chosen as the data transfer software.	

Explanation:

Reply suggesting that 'Dart Transfer' be chosen as the data transfer software.

- *This is the **most effective** course of action since Dart Transfer strikes the best balance between cost, transfer rate, error rate, and security facilities.*

Reply suggesting that 'Runsfer' be chosen as the data transfer software.

- *This is not the most effective course of action since Runsfer does not offer the same amount of security features, and has a slower transfer rate than Dart Transfer.*

Reply suggesting that 'Library Ladder Transfer Solution' be chosen as the data transfer software.

- *This is not the most effective course of action since it has a slow transfer rate and offers little security features.*

Reply suggesting that 'Super Speed Transfer' be chosen as the data transfer software.

- *This is not the most effective course of action since it costs the most, and has the least security features.*

Task 2

Choose the **most effective** and **least effective** course of action:

	Most Effective	Least Effective
Assign Oliver IT tasks.		✓
Have Oliver act as a liaison between yourself and the rest of the team.		
Assign Oliver the task of writing a report explaining what the plan for the enrolment project is, writing regular updates for your manager to read.	✓	
Place Oliver in a position so that he can work closely with Lily and develop his IT skills.		

Explanation:

Assign Oliver the task of writing a report explaining what the plan for the enrolment project is, writing regular updates for your manager to read.

- *This is the **most effective** course of action since it best suits Oliver's skillset as a legislative and PR writer.*

Assign Oliver IT tasks.

- *This is the **least effective** course of action since IT is Oliver's main development area. While it's important to help cultivate his skills and help him improve, setting Oliver to work on these tasks on such an important project would not be an effective use of his skills.*

Have Oliver act as a liaison between yourself and the rest of the team.

- *This is not a particularly effective course of action since you shouldn't require a liaison between yourself and your team – you should be speaking with each of them directly. Likewise, it doesn't entirely utilise Oliver's skills.*

Place Oliver in a position so that he can work closely with Lily and develop his IT skills.

- *This is a somewhat effective course of action. On one hand, you are giving Lily and Oliver both a chance to develop their skills by working together. However, there is a lot of work to be done and therefore it isn't the most effective course of action since it may be quite time-consuming.*

Task 3

Choose the **most effective** course of action:

Read the data protection policy document before replying to Cynthia to confirm that you have read and understand the rules and guidelines.	
Reply to Cynthia, informing her that you have read and understand the rules and guidelines, before reading the data protection policy later in your own time.	
Read the data protection policy document, as well as the Data Protection Act, before replying to Cynthia to confirm that you have read and understand the rules and guidelines.	✓
Ignore the data protection policy document and continue with your work.	

Explanation:

Read the data protection policy document, as well as the Data Protection Act, before replying to Cynthia to confirm that you have read and understand the rules and guidelines.

- *This is the **most effective** course of action since you are being as thorough as possible when it comes to understanding the rules regarding data protection. Since you're going to be leading a team on a project which heavily involves data handling, it's vital that you are as aware as possible about data protection laws and policy.*

Read the data protection policy document before replying to Cynthia to confirm that you have read and understand the rules and guidelines.

- *While this is an adequate response, you are only completing the task at its bare minimum. Since you're leading a team on a project involving data handling, it is important that you know as much as possible about data protection. Therefore, you could go an extra step and read about the Data Protection Act.*

Reply to Cynthia, informing her that you have read and understand the rules and guidelines, before reading the data protection policy later in your own time.

- *This is not an effective response because you are lying to Cynthia. While it's understandable to want to read more about the data protection policy in your own time, it's important that you complete the task set for you before the deadline. Likewise, it's important not to lie to your manager.*

Ignore the data protection policy document and continue with your work.

- *This is not an effective response because you are disobeying a request made by your manager. Understanding data protection law and data protection policy is a fundamental part of this project, and so to ignore this responsibility would run counter to your job.*

Task 4

Choose the **most effective** and **least effective** course of action:

	Most Effective	Least Effective
Reply to the letter, asking to meet with Carl, your team member, and his team member.		
Reply to the letter, asking Carl to give you the name of the team member who was breaking these rules. Meet with this team member privately and discuss the issue with them before taking it further.	✓	
Contact your manager and ask her what she thinks you should do.		
Hold a meeting with your entire team asking the person who broke the rules to come forward.		✓

Explanation:

Reply to the letter, asking Carl to give you the name of the team member who was breaking these rules. Meet with this team member privately and discuss the issue with them before taking it further.

- *This is the **most effective** course of action since you are addressing the issue as soon and as directly as possible. Data protection is a serious issue, and so it makes sense to get in touch with the team member and find out their side of the story before proceeding.*

Hold a meeting with your entire team asking the person who broke the rules to come forward.

- *This is the **least effective** course of action because there's no guarantee that the person will admit to their wrongdoing in front of everyone. It would be far more effective to get the name of the person from Carl, and speak to them directly.*

Reply to the letter, asking to meet with Carl, your team member, and his team member.

- *This is a somewhat effective response. However, there's no need to get Carl and the accuser involved immediately. It's much better to speak to the accused first and find out what their side of the story is.*

Contact your manager and ask her what she thinks you should do.

- *This is an ineffective course of action because you need to be able to handle this situation yourself. If you run into issues later on, you can discuss with your manager. However, there is already a clear course of action set.*

Task 5

Choose the **most effective** and **least effective** course of action:

	Most Effective	Least Effective
Reply to Megan, asking for her to lend you some additional computers for the project.		
Ignore the email. There's no need for any correspondence at this time.		✓
Reply to Megan to confirm that you will contact her if any extra computers are needed. You also confirm that you will grant her access to the software once it has been purchased and installed.	✓	
Ask Lily to reply to Megan's letter.		

Explanation:

Reply to Megan to confirm that you will contact her if any extra computers are needed. You also confirm that you will grant her access to the software once it has been purchased and installed.

- *This is the **most effective** response since you are replying to show Megan that you have read her letter.*

Ignore the email. There's no need for any correspondence at this time.

- *This is the **least effective** response because you aren't giving Megan any indication that you've read what she has sent to you.*

Reply to Megan, asking for her to lend you some additional computers for the project.

- *This is not a particularly effective response because you do not yet know how many machines you will need.*

Ask Lily to reply to Megan's letter.

* *This is an ineffective response since, although you're demonstrating that you've read the letter, you aren't replying to Megan directly. You're taking time away from Lily which could be better spent on another task.*

Now, have a go at our next In-Tray exercise. Unlike the previous, this is a mock-up of the real thing! Once you've read through everything, put your recommendations and priorities into the form of a written letter:

Sample In-Tray Exercise 2

Background Information:

You are a new Detective Constable at Ficshire Police. You only recently finished your probationary period in another city, and now you have been relocated to Ficshire.

As a Detective Constable, you are in charge of managing and leading a team of police officers and other workers. Your team consists of the following:

- **PC Martin.** PC Martin has been with the police for 2 years now. She is experienced, dependable and gets along with everyone in the team.

- **PC Andrews.** PC Andrews is the oldest member of the team. He is frequently grumpy with your other colleagues, and isn't particularly popular.

- **Janet Edwards.** Janet takes care of the admin side of things for your department. Janet takes Mondays off, as she also cares for her disabled sister.

- **DC Richards.** DC Richards is an experienced Detective Constable, who has been assigned to help you out this week.

- **Ben Smith.** Ben is a trainee admin assistant, who is working with your team. He only started working this week.

Document 1

**FICSHIRE POLICE
SERVICE**

Ficshire Police Department
1 Ficshire Way,
Ficshire,
F00 0FC

-- -- ,

I'd like to take the opportunity to welcome you to the team. We are confident that you will be a fantastic addition to our policing team, and we're all looking forward to working with you.

I know you only started this week, but unfortunately we're going to be dropping you straight in the deep-end! DC Parish is away for the next week or so, since his wife has just had a baby, so you'll need to help out with his tasks. All of the emails and letters have been forwarded to you, so take a look at these and work out how you are going to prioritise them, and how you intend to resolve them.

Once you're done looking at everything, email me back a written response on how you'll go about resolving it all!

Best of luck,
Chief Inspector Starkey.

Ficshire Police Service

Ficshire Police Department | 1 Ficshire Way, Ficshire, F00 0FC

Document 2

18:45: Doors open, seating begins.

19:15: Welcoming speech from various committee members.

19:30: Run down of topics from last meeting, progress update on neighbourhood activity.

20:00: Priority issues discussion/debate amongst attendees.

20:30: Tea break.

20:45: Further debate, recommendations to be made on how to resolve ongoing issues.

21:00: Guest speaker from Ficville City Police department.

21:45: Organising next meeting, handing out an action plan to attendees.

Document 3

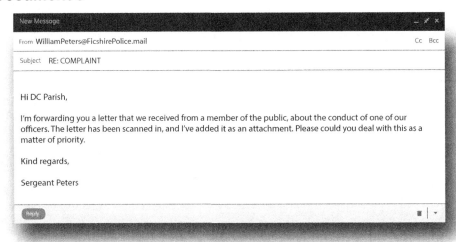

New Message ‒ ✗ ✕

From WilliamPeters@FicshirePolice.mail   Cc Bcc

Subject RE: COMPLAINT

Hi DC Parish,

I'm forwarding you a letter that we received from a member of the public, about the conduct of one of our officers. The letter has been scanned in, and I've added it as an attachment. Please could you deal with this as a matter of priority.

Kind regards,

Sergeant Peters

Reply

---

10 Ficshire Avenue
Ficshire
FOI FC8

Ficshire Police Department
1 Ficshire Way,
Ficshire,
FOO OFC

10th May

COMPLAINT

Dear Sir/Madam,

I am writing to Ficshire Police, as I am quite appalled by the horror of what I witnessed just two days ago. As you know, elections were taking place earlier this week, and there has been a great deal of conflict in this town between the two leading parties. On the day in question, I was working at Ficshire Town Hall. I was asked to attend the town hall to oversee the election process, and make sure everything went smoothly.

There were police from your station already at the scene, to make sure everything went smoothly. Halfway through the day, with no sign of violence, everything appeared to be going smoothly...but then. My goodness, the horror. Two men strolled through the door, holding hands! I could not believe my eyes. The sheer gall of it. I immediately asked the officer in charge to escort the men from the premises and throw them into a cell, where hopefully they would rot. The officer in question absolutely refused to do this. He told me that I was being discriminatory and homophobic, and allowed them to vote. Following this, they left.

This is truly disgusting and I hope that you will reprimand the officer in question. His name was PC Davies, and I demand that he is stripped of all responsibility and handed over to the government for interrogation. I sincerely hope that this man's views do not reflect those of our law enforcement institutions.

Yours sincerely,

Luke Bellamy,
Civil Servant, Advocator for Social Change, and loyal servant of the crown.

Document 4

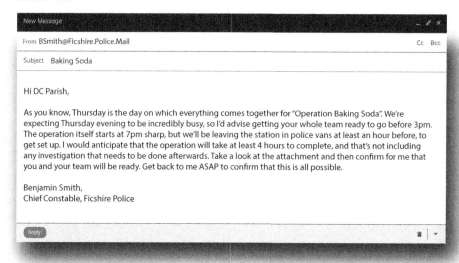

> New Message _ ✗ ✗
>
> From BSmith@Ficshire.Police.Mail   Cc   Bcc
>
> Subject   Baking Soda
>
> Hi DC Parish,
>
> As you know, Thursday is the day on which everything comes together for "Operation Baking Soda". We're expecting Thursday evening to be incredibly busy, so I'd advise getting your whole team ready to go before 3pm. The operation itself starts at 7pm sharp, but we'll be leaving the station in police vans at least an hour before, to get set up. I would anticipate that the operation will take at least 4 hours to complete, and that's not including any investigation that needs to be done afterwards. Take a look at the attachment and then confirm for me that you and your team will be ready. Get back to me ASAP to confirm that this is all possible.
>
> Benjamin Smith,
> Chief Constable, Ficshire Police
>
> Reply   🗑 ┆ ▾

OPERATION BAKING SODA

Operation Baking Soda is a multi-agency operation developed by Ficshire Police and Ficville City Police, with the aiming of detaining a notorious drug syndicate, that operates between the two districts. Officers from both police forces, as well as government agencies, have been monitoring the progress of the syndicate for over a year. Now, it has been agreed that the time is right to strike.

On Thursday 12th July at 19:00, officers from both forces will congregate discreetly in the alcove separating Ficshire Arcade from the beach. It is believed that an enormous drug deal will be taking place, and the opportunity will be had to make major arrests. As a result, both Ficshire Police and Ficville City Police are deploying major resources to the area. This will include armed officers, in anticipation of the suspects resisting arrest.

Document 5

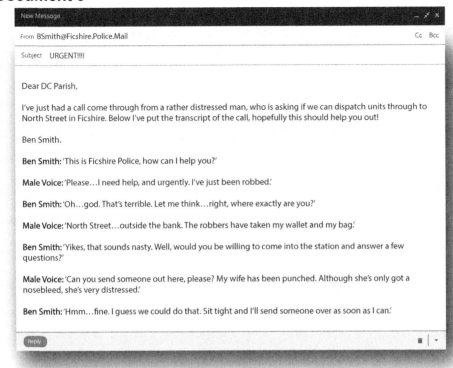

New Message — ⤢ ×

From BSmith@Ficshire.Police.Mail   Cc Bcc

Subject   URGENT!!!!

Dear DC Parish,

I've just had a call come through from a rather distressed man, who is asking if we can dispatch units through to North Street in Ficshire. Below I've put the transcript of the call, hopefully this should help you out!

Ben Smith.

Ben Smith: 'This is Ficshire Police, how can I help you?'

Male Voice: 'Please…I need help, and urgently. I've just been robbed.'

Ben Smith: 'Oh…god. That's terrible. Let me think…right, where exactly are you?'

Male Voice: 'North Street…outside the bank. The robbers have taken my wallet and my bag.'

Ben Smith: 'Yikes, that sounds nasty. Well, would you be willing to come into the station and answer a few questions?'

Male Voice: 'Can you send someone out here, please? My wife has been punched. Although she's only got a nosebleed, she's very distressed.'

Ben Smith: 'Hmm…fine. I guess we could do that. Sit tight and I'll send someone over as soon as I can.'

Reply

Start writing your report in the textbox below, and see what you can come up with.

Surprise, you've got new mail! Unfortunately, your report just isn't going to cut it now, so take a look at the emails below and now work them into a new report, again prioritising the key issues. This is something that will actually occur during your real test, so you need to be able to think on your feet!

Document 6

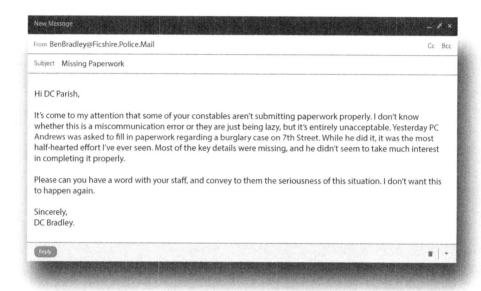

New Message

From BenBradley@Ficshire.Police.Mail

Cc   Bcc

Subject   Missing Paperwork

Hi DC Parish,

It's come to my attention that some of your constables aren't submitting paperwork properly. I don't know whether this is a miscommunication error or they are just being lazy, but it's entirely unacceptable. Yesterday PC Andrews was asked to fill in paperwork regarding a burglary case on 7th Street. While he did it, it was the most half-hearted effort I've ever seen. Most of the key details were missing, and he didn't seem to take much interest in completing it properly.

Please can you have a word with your staff, and convey to them the seriousness of this situation. I don't want this to happen again.

Sincerely,
DC Bradley.

Reply

Document 7

Hi DC Parish,

Unfortunately, I am going to have to tender my resignation. Due to circumstances at home, with my sister, I simply can't continue working full-time. I would like to arrange a meeting with you at your earliest convenience, so that we can discuss this further. Of course, I wanted to give you full notice beforehand. I have really enjoyed working here, and the opportunity has been incredible.

Please get back to me as soon as possible.

Thank you,

Janet Edwards

Document 8

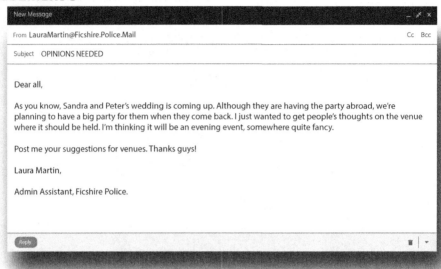

New Message _ ⤢ ×

From LauraMartin@Ficshire.Police.Mail   Cc   Bcc

Subject   OPINIONS NEEDED

Dear all,

As you know, Sandra and Peter's wedding is coming up. Although they are having the party abroad, we're planning to have a big party for them when they come back. I just wanted to get people's thoughts on the venue where it should be held. I'm thinking it will be an evening event, somewhere quite fancy.

Post me your suggestions for venues. Thanks guys!

Laura Martin,

Admin Assistant, Ficshire Police.

Reply   🗑 | ▾

Now, write a report to your Chief Constable, detailing how you would deal with all of this, and showing how you'd go about prioritising the various issues.

Sample Report

Dear Inspector Stanley,

I am writing to you with my recommendations on how the issues raised should be dealt with, and in which priority they should be accounted for.

My immediate priority in this case would be to deal with the email from Ben Smith. The reason I have chosen this as my first priority, is because it concerns a crime which has only just occurred. The victim has requested an immediate callout. Although it would appear that we are too late to stop the crime from happening, if we send officers to the scene immediately then we will lower the chance of key evidence becoming lost or damaged, as well as showing the individuals concerned that the police can be relied on to deal with incidents like this. Furthermore, this is a priority because Ben Smith has clearly not behaved in an acceptable manner. Although he is a new trainee, he needs to be shown that his phone manner is not conducive to good police work. I noticed that in the transcript, he failed to reassure the victim, and in general did not project any confidence. So, after I have dispatched officers for immediate dispatch to the scene, I would find Ben and have a talk with him about the way he is dealing with calls such as this in the future – as he can't be allowed to make the same mistakes again. Professionalism is extremely important for police employees, and in this case Ben has clearly exhibited a serious lack of this.

The next issue on my list, would be Operation Baking Soda. I would reply to Chief Constable Benjamin Smith (not to be confused with trainee admin assistant Ben Smith) in order to confirm the plans for this operation. This is because the Chief Constable requested that I get back to him ASAP. Given the significance of this operation, it goes without saying that we need to organise our resources as effectively as possible. Getting everything in place early will go a long way to doing this, and ensuring that everyone understands their role in the operation.

In conjunction with the above, provided I have the time, I would make attempts to see whether there were any other members of staff available who could attend Paul Wiggins's neighbourhood watch meeting. If not, then I would reply directly to Paul, informing him that DC Parish is away, and that we wouldn't be able to attend this meeting due to other essential police issues. The meeting takes place at the same time as Operation Baking Soda, and obviously the operation needs to be given priority. Naturally I wouldn't disclose the details of the operation to Paul, I'd just tell him that it's urgent police business. However, I would try and assure him that we'd make an attempt to come next time, and that we really value the feedback of the community in our work. I would also inform Paul that I'd be happy to receive any feedback from the meeting in the form of a letter, which the constabulary would then endeavour to respond to as soon as possible.

Next, there are two issues – Janet Edwards's resignation, and the letter from DC Bradley. These are both serious issues, but I would give priority to Janet Edwards in this case. The reason I would give this priority is that this is something which could be resolved fairly quickly. I'd immediately approach Janet to discuss the issue. Obviously, I am not the person with whom she would be tendering her resignation, but I could definitely arrange for her to meet with a senior member of staff. I believe this is important, as it will give her peace of mind, and as a result she will work more efficiently and effectively in the time that she has remaining with Ficshire Police.

As for the letter with DC Bradley, this is something I would take very seriously. Before approaching the staff, however, I would see if I can meet with DC Bradley one to one to discuss the issue and get the exact details. Following this, I'd make arrangements to meet with the relevant members of my team, and enquire as to why they behaved in this way, and to ensure that this doesn't happen in the future.

The penultimate priority on my list would be to reply to the letter from Luke Bellamy. I would give this very short shrift, as he is clearly in the wrong. In my letter, I would tell Mr Bellamy that the police do not tolerate any form of discrimination, and that I was proud of my officer for behaving in the way that he did, and that I hoped our staff would all behave this way in the future. In the event that a member of the public behaves like this, we should take responsibility for educating them and showing them that their behaviour is wrong.

Finally, and only if I had the time, I might reply to the email from Laura Martin, if I could think of a suggested location off the top of my head. Obviously it's always polite to take the feelings of your colleagues into consideration, but this would naturally be the last item on my list – as it doesn't require an immediate response, and certainly shouldn't be placed above any normal police work.

Briefing Exercise

Following your In-Tray assessment, you will be asked to take what is known as a Briefing exercise.

The Briefing exercise lasts for around 1 hour in total. You'll likely be given 30 minutes before the exercise to prepare, and 30 minutes to complete the exercise itself. During the exercise, you will be asked to give a verbal presentation on the In-Tray exercise, to an inspector. Essentially, you will be physically describing all of the elements that you listed in your In-Tray report.

The presentation normally lasts for 30 minutes overall, with a period of 15 minutes dedicated to presenting and 15 minutes where you will be asked questions by your assessors (your "inspector") based on what you've said. These questions will be focused around the topics that you've raised, and you'll need to provide good quality answers to all of them in order to pass. You will be allowed to bring your report into the Briefing with you, but you'll be judged based on how well you can present your ideas, so it's essential that you can make the most of the planning stage.

As we've mentioned, you will be given a period of 30 minutes prior to the exercise, to plan how you will present your ideas to the inspector. With this in mind, here are some tips on how to go about acing this exercise

Think About The Implications of Your Decisions

When you go into the briefing exercise, you will need to give clear rationale for every single decision that you've made. With this in mind, a good thing to do during the planning stage is to create a numbered list. So, you could start with number 1 – your first priority:

Priority 1 – Email from Ben Smith

Underneath this, write down your reasoning for making this the first priority. Try to think of as many reasons as you can for why it's important. Then, decide how you are going to deal with it.

As a Detective Constable, you will be expected to read between the lines. This is part of the core competency of having an investigative mind. You must be someone who can think beyond simple explanations and solutions, and find creative and innovative fixes to problems. That being said, sometimes the simplest solution is the right one. In the case of this particular issue, there isn't anything complex about it. You need to send a team of officers to deal with the situation ASAP.

TIP: *Look out for connections between the different scenarios - are some of the reports or crimes related?*

Consider the structure of your response

During the briefing, you will be talking for a good 15 minutes. This is a long time to talk, even though it probably won't feel like it once you are actually speaking. It's very easy to get carried away and start rambling, giving the inspector a messy and unstructured response. It's imperative that you can properly structure your response, as this will help to make your ideas clear to the inspector. The clearer your response, the better you will score, and the more logical your ideas will come across.

Generally, you should structure your response in the same way that you did your letter – starting with the highest priority, and then moving through the different issues, until you finish with the lowest priority.

Competencies

The Briefing exercise will test you on the following competencies:

- Team Working;
- Positive Drive;
- Resilience;
- Communication;
- Professional Approach;
- Learning.

As always, the competencies will play a vital role in how you are scored for this exercise. Factor the competencies into your responses – call them by name e.g. it's important that our officers show professionalism when dealing with members of the public. The better you can do this, the higher marks you will get.

Plan for questions

You can't predict exactly what the investigator is going to ask you, but it's always good to have a think about what types of questions you'll be asked. This will ensure that you aren't caught off guard by anything, and can give clear and direct responses. Here are some potential questions that you should try and be ready for:

- Why have you prioritised [x scenario] over [y scenario]?

- How confident are you in this course of action?

- How do you think this decision will impact the community?

- What will you do if .... happens?

- How can we trust you to take this approach?

- Do you think the police have the resources to accommodate this action?

The questions won't just be focused on your suggestions, but also on your integrity, confidence and ability to carry out the recommended course of action. You might also be asked questions about your responses to the original questions. For example, if the inspector asks, 'How do you think this will impact the community?' and your response is to tell them that you feel it will have a positive impact on the community because *A*, *B* and *C* then they might ask, 'Well, what about *D*?'

Posture Matters!

If you've ever performed a presentation before, then you'll be aware that how you physically present yourself to the room can make a big difference. You need to project an air of confidence, without coming across as brash and arrogant. The more confident you appear, the more confident the inspector will be in your ideas and opinions. Remember that this exercise is just as much about convincing the police that you can make big decisions and that they should have faith in you, as it is actually producing a good report.

Although you are allowed to bring the report into the room with you, you should do your absolute best during the planning stage to try and learn it off by heart. You don't want to be constantly referring back to your notes whilst speaking, as this will look unprofessional and disorganised. When planning your briefing, just as you did before, put each issue under a separate number according to priority. Underneath each point, write down the main issues in a brief list. This will act as an excellent visual cue for the briefing exercise, as you can quickly glance down and see the issue, before looking up and speaking about it in detail.

Before you enter the room, check yourself over in the mirror. Straighten your tie (if wearing one), make sure your shirt is tucked in. Put your shoulders back and walk into the room with your head held high.

Answering Questions

When it comes to answering questions, you'll need to do this in the correct way. It's okay to take a moment to think before speaking, as you consider what has been asked. Don't just rush into an answer without considering the question first, because if you don't answer properly then this will show that you aren't a good listener, and that you don't pay enough attention to detail – both of which are core qualities for Detective Constables to have!

Remember to look the person who is asking you the question in the eye, and speak clearly and slowly so that they can understand you. Leave a pause after each answer, to invite the opportunity for further questioning based on your response.

Closing It Out

Your manners are key to this exercise. Once you've finished giving your briefing, you should close with a statement such as, 'Thank you for very much for listening to my recommendations. I am now happy to answer any questions that you might have.' Before you leave the room at the end of the exercise, thank the inspector again for their time.

Direct Entry Assessment Centre: Interview

The final stage of the day 1 assessment centre is a competency-based interview. During this interview, you will face questions focused around the core competencies for Direct Entry. The core competencies that you will be tested on during the interview, and that you will need to prepare for, are:

- Communication

- Positive Drive

- Resilience

- Emotional Awareness

- Team Working

How Will These Competencies Be Used?

During the interview you will face at least one question based on each of these competencies. You will notice that there are only 5 competencies on this list, which is a really good thing for you! This means that you should be able to come into the interview with a very clear idea of what questions you'll be asked, and how you are going to answer. As we have already explained (in the application form section), competency-based questions focus around past examples of when you've demonstrated said behaviour. They require you to give a structured response, using the STAR method to illustrate how and why you behaved as you did.

In this chapter, we'll help you to practice answering competency based questions.

Other Questions

Along with practicing for the competency-based questions, you also need to prepare answers to 'motivational and values' questions. These will not be present during the assessment centre interview, but there is a good chance that if you are successful over day 1 and 2 of the centre, you will be invited to take part in a more personal interview with ranking officers from your local force. Not all forces will ask you to do this, but it's entirely possible that some will, so you need to be prepared for this.

Motivational and values questions are essentially questions which focus around your reasoning for joining the police, and test your research and commitment to the cause. In this chapter, we'll provide you with lots of sample motivational questions and answers.

Preparing For The Competency-Based Questions

As we've mentioned, the competency-based questions will be centred around the core competencies of team working, positive drive, resilience, emotional awareness and communication. When you prepare for these questions, make sure you have a copy of our core competencies chapter next to you. You need to take into account all of the micro factors that make up these behaviours. For example, 'team working' is not just about working as a member of a team. It's about communicating with your team, being a supportive person, asking for helping, showing understanding and consideration for the feelings of others, and being a leader. So, when you give a response showing that you are a good team worker, take care to show these qualities.

When the assessors question you, they won't always make it so easy. While it's true that some questions will be pretty black and white, for example, 'Give us an example of when you have worked as part of a team to resolve an issue', they may also try and make it a bit more difficult. For some questions, you'll need to take a moment and think about what competency would apply in this scenario. For example, 'Give us an example of a time when you have overcome adversity in the workplace.' You'll notice that the wording of this question doesn't actually incorporate any of the competencies. When you get a question like this, consider the main issue. In this case, the words 'overcome adversity' would be the main topic of the question – which can be linked with resilience.

Now, let's look at some sample competency questions. We've given you a broad mix of easy and tough questions here. After each response, we've included a sample answer, and a space for you to write your own answer.

Q1. Tell us about a time when you have used your communication skills to resolve a difficult problem.

This is a pretty simple one to answer. The question is giving you a clear indication of which competency to use – communication. When answering this, think about all of the aspects that go into 'good communication'. How did you demonstrate these? What did you do specifically that amended the situation, and how did it change things?

Write your answer in the box below, and then compare it to our sample response.

Sample Response

"In my previous role, I worked as a team leader at a catering company. The company had a great reputation, and are well-known nationally. Our company would be paid to organise the catering for parties and events, with different events being given to different teams within the organisation. As one of the team leaders, my role was to oversee the management of any projects that my team was given. This included making sure that the budget was kept to, motivating staff to perform at their best, and giving my team instructions on how we should allocate our resources. In order to help me manage the team, I had assigned a sub-team leader, named Michelle. Michelle would essentially act as my deputy, and would be given responsibility for taking key decisions.

On the day in question, we were preparing for an event in Wolverhampton. The event in question was a big birthday party. I sent my team to the venue to help start setting up, whilst I met with the person who was running the event, just to crosscheck on key elements such as time, and food allergy requirements. When I arrived at the venue, I found that two members of the team were engaged in a furious debate. One of them was Michelle. Voices were being raised and things were getting extremely heated. This was attracting the attention of the venue staff, who looked extremely unimpressed by the situation.

I quickly stepped across, and asked Michelle and the other team member to calm down and come with me outside, so that we could resolve this. I then calmly and professionally asked them to explain what the issue was. Michelle explained to me that the team member in question was refusing to obey her instructions. She had asked him to lay out a series of fish pasties across the table on the right-hand side, but he had refused. Upon hearing this, the team member furiously interrupted. He said that we shouldn't be serving fish pasties, because some attendees would be allergic to fish. He referred to Michelle in extremely demeaning terms. Having spoken with the event manager, I was fully aware of all allergy requirements – and none of the attendees were allergic to fish.

After listening to the complaints, I first addressed the team member. I explained to him that the way he had spoken to Michelle was completely unacceptable, and that even if she had made a mistake then this would not be okay. I then explained to him that he was in fact wrong, and there were no attendees who were allergic. To back this up, I showed him the event listing, which contained the details of all known allergies.

Once the team member saw this, he acknowledged that he had made a mistake, and apologised profusely to Michelle. He begged me not to fire him. Michelle immediately accepted his apology, and informed him that mistakes happen, and that the important thing is to move forward and resolve this. I was happy with this, and authorised the team member to get back to work.

Following this, I spoke to Michelle and informed her that I was pleased with how she dealt with the situation, and that she was doing a great job."

Q2. Can you give an example of a time when you have motivated a colleague to improve their performance?

This question requires you to think a bit more about which competency is relevant. Which of the competencies requires you to motivate your colleagues and encourage them to improve? The core competency required here is positive drive. Positive drive is about having the drive and commitment to uphold the highest possible standards, whilst maintaining a positive and enthusiastic outlook on your work. This is also a good opportunity for you to show your leadership skills!

Write your answer in the box below, and then compare it to our sample response.

Sample Response

"Whilst working in my previous role, as a sales assistant in a computer shop, I was required to use my technical expertise on a number of occasions.

One such incident occurred on a regular weekday. A customer had come into the store, to complain that the laptop he'd brought from us two months earlier, had crashed. The customer did not have warranty on this laptop. My colleague, who was new to the role, was assigned to deal with the customer.

Unfortunately, my colleague made a mistake, which resulted in the customer becoming very angry. In response, my colleague was very rude to the customer, demonstrating very poor customer handling skills. After stepping in to defuse this situation, I apologised wholeheartedly on behalf of the store and offered the customer a full refund, or a replacement laptop, and he seemed happy with this.

Once the customer had left the store, I took my colleague to one side. He was extremely upset by the incident, and felt that he had let down our employers. I encouraged him not to feel upset about the incident, and advised him to closely read over the store terms and conditions, so that mistakes like this wouldn't happen again. However, I noticed that he did not seem to understand that he had been rude to the customer.

Upon further exploration of this, I found out that the individual in question had had almost zero customer service training before being placed on the shop floor, and this was likely the reason for his poor communication. I immediately explained to him exactly why his behaviour was poor, and why customer service is so essential. I told him that he was a representative of the shop, and that the shop's reputation would be damaged by behaviour such as this. I also explained that we have a duty to customers to be polite and respectful at all times, even if we do not agree with what the customer is saying. Finally, I reassured him that I was confident in his ability to do the job, and would always be here to help if he needed advice.

Following this incident, I noticed a marked increase in my colleague's behaviour. The next time he was placed in such a situation, he remained calm and composed, and exhibited a good level of service towards the customer."

Q3. Can you give me an example of a time when you have done what you believed was right, even when others disagreed with you?

If you look at this question closely, you'll notice that it's referring to the core competency of resilience. Be careful though, because there is a fine line between stubbornness and resilience. When you explain to the interviewer what happened, make sure you choose a situation where your instincts were right, and where there was clear protocol behind your decision.

Write your answer in the box below, and then compare it to our sample response.

Sample Response

"Whilst working in my current position as a sales person, I was the duty manager for the day, as my manager had gone sick. It was the week before Christmas and the shop was very busy.

During the day the fire alarm went off, and I started to ask everybody to evacuate the shop, which is our company policy. The alarm has gone off in the past but the normal manager usually lets people stay in the shop whilst he finds out if it's a false alarm.

This was a difficult situation because the shop was very busy, nobody wanted to leave and my shop assistants were disagreeing with me in my decision to evacuate the shop. Some of the customers were becoming irate as they were in the changing rooms at the time. The customers were saying that it was appalling that they had to evacuate the shop and that they would complain to the head office about it. The sales staff were trying to persuade me to keep everybody inside the shop, and saying that it was most probably a false alarm as usual. I was determined to evacuate everybody from the shop for safety reasons, and would not allow anybody to deter me from my aim. The safety of my staff and customers was at the forefront of my mind, even though it wasn't at theirs.

Whilst remaining calm and in control, I shouted at the top of my voice that everybody was to leave, even though the sound of the alarm was reducing the impact of my voice. I then had to instruct my staff to walk around the shop and tell everybody to leave whilst we investigated the problem. I had to inform one member of staff that disciplinary action would be taken against him if he did not co-operate. Eventually, after I kept persisting, everybody began to leave the shop. I then went outside with my members of staff, took a roll call and awaited the Fire Brigade to arrive.

At first I felt a little apprehensive and under pressure, but was determined not to move from my position, as I knew 100% that it was the right one. I was disappointed that my staff did not initially help me, but the more I persisted the more confident I became. Eventually the Fire Brigade showed up, and they discovered that there was in fact a small fire at the back of the store. Luckily nobody was harmed, but the consequences could have been severe if I hadn't got everyone out.

This was the first time I had been the manager of the shop so I felt that this situation tested my courage and determination. By remaining calm I was able to deal with the situation far more effectively. I now felt that I had the courage to manage the shop better and had proven to myself that I was capable of dealing with difficult situations. I had learnt that staying calm under pressure improves your chances of a successful outcome dramatically."

Q4. Can you give me an example of a time when you have demonstrated empathy and understanding towards another person's difficulties?

The qualities listed in this question fall under the competency of 'emotional awareness'. Again, make sure that you look through the list of competencies, to see which match up to the qualities listed in the question. Emotional awareness incorporates your understanding of other people's feelings, and your ability to be sensitive towards colleagues and members of the public. Your response should show that you are a sensitive and compassionate person.

Write your answer in the box below, and then compare it to our sample response.

Sample Response

"During my previous role as an administration manager, at my previous company, I was given leadership of a team of other admin workers. Our responsibilities included dealing with absences from the company, managing the finance elements of the business, and making appointments for the management team.

As the leader of the team, one of my jobs was to make sure that new staff to the department felt welcomed and integrated. On the week in question, we had two new staff members. One of them, named Eileen, was ultra-confident. She seemed very happy to take on any new tasks, and was happy to work independently. The other new staff member, named Maisie, was less confident. She seemed extremely nervous, and I got the impression that she would need quite a lot of help integrating to the department.

Although I very much wanted to keep an eye on both of them, I decided that I wanted to prioritise Maisie. Therefore, I asked another staff member if they would be happy to oversee Eileen's initial training – just to make sure that she was getting on okay. I then sat down with Maisie myself, to talk with her about integrating into the company. I calmly and professionally discussed her feelings about joining the company, about the work that she'd be doing, and the parts that she felt least confident about. Maisie confessed to me that she felt extremely nervous about the work, and didn't feel confident at all. I informed her that I totally understand her feelings, and assured her that it's completely normal to be nervous when you first start at a company.

Upon establishing which parts she was the least confident in, I put together an action plan. This included training on certain areas, and I also offered to run through certain elements of the job with her as she was doing them, to get her confident in the role.

We worked together for a period of three days, after which time Maisie felt confident enough to work on her own. I am pleased to say that she did really well after this, and was an exemplary member of our team."

Q5. Give me an example of a time when you have worked with other team members, to solve a problem?

This is a pretty simple question to answer. Again, the question is being very direct here, it's asking you to give an example of when you've used team work. Think about the qualities that go into a good team worker – communication, leadership, taking responsibility, and supporting your colleagues. Try and put these into your response.

Write your answer in the box below, and then compare it to our sample response.

Sample Response

"Whilst working for my previous company, as a member of the events team, I was part of the group responsible for managing and organising company conferences. In order to do this, we would have to make contact with the owners of the venue, as well as our client, and negotiate factors such as cost, availability and catering.

The event in question was to be a large-scale conference. Our client was an international refurbishment company, who were running the conference in order to enhance their business network. There were going to be over 500 people attending this conference, from all around the world, so it was essential that we got it right!

The first thing I did was to contact the manager of our client company. I asked him to provide me with a list of every single attendee, where they were travelling from, and whether they would have any special requirements. After the manager sent this through, I split the list into 5 separate parts – with 100 people being sent to 5 different teams within our department. I felt that this was the best approach to managing such a huge number of people. At all times, we liased with the other teams, to make sure everyone was on the right track.

Next, I contacted another department in our company, who were in charge of dealing with issues such as reviews and feedback. I asked them to provide me with the feedback we'd had on our past events, so that I could make sure we did the same things right, and improved on any weak areas. Once they provided me with this list, I made it a priority to improve on the areas which had received negative feedback.

Following the event, which was a huge success, I arranged a meeting with the manager of our client company, to get their thoughts on how the event was run. I wanted to make sure that we worked with this client, in a collaborative fashion, to run future events. The client seemed very happy with how the event was run, and provided us with sustained feedback – which we took into account for the future."

Now that we've covered the competency section, let's have a look at some motivations and values questions.

Motivations And Values Questions

As mentioned, you will not be asked motivations and values questions at the assessment centre. However, if you pass, then there is a good chance that you will be asked to attend a 'final interview' with your local force. The final interview is a great chance for the assessors to get to know you a bit better, and further understand your reasoning for applying to the police. This is important for the police, as they need to be sure that you are applying for the right reasons. They do not want candidates who will drop out within the first few weeks, because the candidate's family are at odds with the decision to join, or because working for the police wasn't what they expected.

The motivations and values questions will be more familiar to most people than competency-based questions. You'll be asked questions such as, 'Why have you applied to join Direct Entry?' 'What do you think makes a good Detective Constable?', 'What is your biggest strength/weakness?' and other common forms of interview question. At all points, be honest with the interviewers.

Below we've listed some sample questions and responses to this section. Write your answer in the box below the question, then compare it with our sample response!

Q1. Tell us about why you have applied for the Direct Entry programme.

In this question, you need to give an honest account of why you've applied. You can fall back on your research here. Are there any specific qualities of the programme which interest you? If so, which, and why? Try and link your character and background to the programme too. Think about your history and what motivated you to apply.

Write your answer in the box below, and then compare it to our sample response.

Sample Response

"I feel that the Direct Entry programme represents a fantastic opportunity. I have always been interested in pursuing a career with the police, and I can distinctly remember the time I decided this would be the job for me. I was walking through my local high street on my way to the gym on an early Saturday morning, when I noticed two police officers dealing with an aggressive and verbally abusive young man. The two police officers remained totally calm and in control of the situation, despite the abuse being directed at them by the man. Their body language was non-confrontational, and they appeared to be using established techniques to get him to calm down.

Following this, I conducted significant research into the police, and learned about the role of Detective Constable. Immediately this was hugely appealing to me. The idea of taking a lead role in investigations, and working in an organisation that is as established and respected as the police, sounds absolutely fantastic. I am someone who likes to take responsibility, and for most of my career I have worked within leadership positions. With this in mind, I would love the chance to join the police directly as a Detective Constable. I would thrive on the challenge that this brings, and I hope that you will consider me."

Q2. Tell us qualities you believe you have, that will be relevant to the role of a Detective Constable.

In your response here, think about what qualities would make a good Detective Constable. Then, link them with your own qualities! Focus on just a few qualities which you think are the strongest, and elaborate on how they would be useful when working in the role.

Write your answer in the box below, and then compare it to our sample response.

Sample Response

"To begin with, I am a hard-working, committed and highly-motivated person who prides himself on the ability to continually learn and develop new skills. I am 31 years old, and I currently work as a customer services manager for a transportation company. In addition to being a family person, I also have my own hobbies and interests, which include team sports such as football and also playing the guitar in a local band.

I am a loyal person, who has a strong track record at work for being reliable, flexible and customer-focused. My annual appraisals are consistently to a high standard and I am always willing to learn new skills. Before applying for this job, I studied the role of a Detective Constable and also the role of the police service in depth, to make sure I was able to meet the requirements of the role. Having been working for my current employer for almost ten years now, I wanted to make sure that I had the potential to become a competent employee of the police before applying. Job stability is important to me and my family. If successful, I plan to stay in the police force for many years."

Q3. Tell us what work you have done during your preparation for applying to become a Detective Constable.

The police will want to know that you've conducted thorough preparation before applying. They want to see a level of dedication and enthusiasm right from the outset, and not just when you've got the job. Don't be surprised to encounter a question such as this, which directly challenges the amount of work you've put in beforehand. Remember too that there is enormous competition for a place on the Direct Entry course. All of the other candidates (or the good ones anyway) will have put in strong amounts of preparation work beforehand – so you need to do your utmost to top this.

Write your answer in the box below, and then compare it to our sample response.

Sample Response

"I have carried out a huge amount of work, research and personal development prior to applying for this role. To begin with, I studied the role of a Detective Constable, especially with regards to the core competencies. I wanted to make sure that I could meet the requirements of the role, so I asked myself whether I had sufficient evidence and experience to match each and every one of the core competencies.

Once I was certain that I had the experience in life, I started to find out more about the work that Detective Constables carry out. I have studied your local force's website in detail, and learnt as much as I possibly could about how you tackle crime, deal with the effects of it and also how you use statistics to drive down increasing crime trends in specific areas. In addition to reading and researching, I went along to my local police station to try and find out a bit more about the job, and the expectations that the public have from the police."

Q4. Tell us about what your biggest strength is, and how this will benefit the police should we employ you.

This is a very common question, and it's also one that is highly likely to appear during the interview section. When answering this question, be careful. The interviewer will want you to focus on one major strength. They don't want an entire speech on how great you are and all of your qualities. Focus on one major quality, and then elaborate on how you believe this can help in your role as Detective Constable.

Write your answer in the box below, and then compare it to our sample response.

Sample Response

"I believe that my biggest strength is in my ability to take leadership of difficult situations, and make crucial decisions. In my previous career, I have almost always worked in management positions, where I was required to make important decisions on a regular basis. I am well suited to dealing with large amounts of pressure and feel comfortable in making big decisions, as well as taking ownership and responsibility for these judgements.

I believe that this quality will strongly benefit me in my career as a police officer. I understand that as a Detective Constable involves large amounts of high-pressure decision making, and that Detective Constables must be able to remain calm and collected when the going gets tough. I feel that my decision-making skills would transfer over extremely well to the police, and that I would be able to benefit your force in this regard."

Q5. Do you have any questions for us?

This is the final question in most non-competency based interviews, and it's super important that you answer in the right way! At the end of an interview, you should always try to ask the interviewer some questions. The reason for this is that it shows a level of interest in the role, and it shows the interviewer that you are enthusiastic and passionate about progressing. Answering this question with 'no' will leave a poor impression, and could hurt your chances.

Here's some potential questions that you could ask at the end of an interview:

- Can you tell me a bit more about what type of training I'll take during the Direct Entry programme?

- If I am successful in applying for a place, how long will it be before I can start training?

- I understand that there is a two-year probationary period whilst I train to become a Detective Constable. Is it possible to cut this period down, through good performance?

- Do you have any concerns over my ability to do this role?

Assessment Centre: Day 2

Following the first day of the assessment, you will be invited to attend day 2. Day 2 consists of a fitness assessment – known as the bleep test, and various medical/physical checks. Below we've provided you with some information about the fitness assessment, and how to prepare for it:

The Bleep Test

The Bleep Test, otherwise known as the Multi-Stage Fitness Test or the shuttle-run test, is a challenging fitness assessment. When taking part in this exercise, you will need to run continuously between two lines, set 20 metres apart, whilst a series of bleep noises plays in the background. The bleeps tell you when you can run from one line to the other. So, you need to aim to be at the next line before the next bleep sounds.

As the test goes on, the speed of the bleeps increases. If you can't reach the line before the next bleep sounds, then you'll be given a warning. If you fail to reach the line on two consecutive occasions after a warning, then the test will be over for you.

Scoring

Your performance in the bleep test will be scored based on how long you continue the test. Candidates are scored via a levelling system, which is related to how fast the bleeps are at the point where they drop out. In order to pass the fitness assessment, you will need to reach a score of 5.4.

Below we've included some tips, on how to improve your fitness and get in shape for the bleep test.

Running Programme

One of the best ways to prepare for the fitness tests is to embark on a structured running programme.

You do not need to run at a fast pace or even run for long distances, in order to gain massively from this type of exercise. Before we provide you with the running programme however, take a read of the following important running tips.

Tips for running

- As with any exercise you should consult a doctor before taking part to make sure that you are medically fit.

- It is certainly worth investing in a pair of comfortable running shoes that serve the purpose for your intended training programme. Your local sports shop will be able to advise you on the types that are best for you. You don't have to spend a fortune to buy a good pair of running shoes.

- It is a good idea to invest in a 'high visibility' jacket or coat so that you can be seen by fast moving traffic if you intend to run on or near the road.

- Make sure you carry out at least 5 whole minutes of stretching exercises not only before but also after your running programme. This can help to prevent injury.

- Whilst you shouldn't run on a full stomach, it is also not good to run on an empty one either. A great food to eat approximately 30 minutes before a run is a banana. This is great for giving you energy.

- Drink plenty of water throughout the day. Try to drink at least 1.5 litres each day in total. This will keep you hydrated and help to prevent muscle cramp.

- Don't overdo it. If you feel any pain or discomfort then stop and seek medical advice.

Walking at a brisk pace is probably the most effective way to lose weight if you need to. It is possible to burn the same amount of calories if you walk the same distance as if you were running.

When walking at a 'brisk' pace it is recommended that you walk as fast as is comfortably possible without breaking into a run or slow jog.

RUNNING PROGRAMME WEEK 1 DAY 1

- Run a total of 3 miles only at a steady pace. If you cannot manage 3 miles then try the following:

- Walk at a brisk pace for half a mile or approximately 10 minutes.

- Run for 1 mile or 8 minutes.

- Walk for another half a mile or approximately 10 minutes.

- Run for 1.5 miles or 12 minutes.

RUNNING PROGRAMME WEEK 1 DAY 2

- Walk for 2 miles or approximately 20 minutes at a brisk pace.
- Run for 2 miles or 14 minutes.
- Repeat DAY ONE.
- Walk at a brisk pace for 0.5 miles or approximately 7 minutes.
- Run for 3 miles or 20 minutes.

DAY 5

- Repeat day one.

DAY 6 AND DAY 7

- Rest days. No exercise.

RUNNING PROGRAMME WEEK 2 DAY 1

- Run for 4 miles or 25 minutes.

DAY 2

- Run a total of 3 miles at a steady pace.

If you cannot manage 3 miles then try the following:

- Walk at a brisk pace for half a mile or approximately 10 minutes.
- Run for 1 mile or 8 minutes.
- Walk for another half a mile or approximately 10 minutes.
- Run for 1.5 miles or 12 minutes.

RUNNING PROGRAMME WEEK 2 DAY 3

- Rest day. No exercise.

DAY 4

- Run for 5 miles or 35–40 minutes.

DAY 5

- Run for 3 miles or 20 minutes.

- Walk at a brisk pace for 2 miles or approximately 20 minutes.

DAY 6

- Run for 5 miles or 35–45 minutes.

DAY 7

- Rest day. No exercise.

Once you have completed the second week running programme, use the 3rd week to perform different types of exercises, such as cycling and swimming. During week 4 you can then commence the 2-week running programme again. You'll be amazed at how much easier it is the second time around!

When preparing for the selection process, use your exercise time as a break from your studies. For example, if you have been working on the application form for a couple of hours why not take a break and go running? When you return from your run you can then concentrate on your studies feeling refreshed.

Now that we've provided you with a structured running programme to follow, there really are no excuses. So, get out there, start running and start preparing for your fitness assessment!

MORE TITLES THAT WILL HELP YOU PASS THE ASSESSMENT PROCESS!

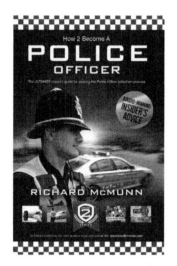

FOR MORE CAREER ADVICE GO TO:
WWW.HOW2BECOME.COM

Attend A Detective Constable Direct Entry Training Course

Book Now At:

www.How2Become.com

Printed in Great Britain
by Amazon

44186660R00079